T0077913

THE
SEVEN
GUARDIANS

Embrace your Fully human and
Fully Divine Self As taught by Yeshua &
Miryam (Jesus & Mary Magdalene)

JACQUELINE FERGUSON

BALBOA.PRESS
A DIVISION OF HAY HOUSE

Copyright © 2021 Jacqueline Ferguson.

All rights reserved. No part of this book may be used or reproduced by any means, graphic, electronic, or mechanical, including photocopying, recording, taping or by any information storage retrieval system without the written permission of the author except in the case of brief quotations embodied in critical articles and reviews.

Balboa Press books may be ordered through booksellers or by contacting:

Balboa Press
A Division of Hay House
1663 Liberty Drive
Bloomington, IN 47403
www.balboapress.com
844-682-1282

Because of the dynamic nature of the Internet, any web addresses or links contained in this book may have changed since publication and may no longer be valid. The views expressed in this work are solely those of the author and do not necessarily reflect the views of the publisher, and the publisher hereby disclaims any responsibility for them.

The author of this book does not dispense medical advice or prescribe the use of any technique as a form of treatment for physical, emotional, or medical problems without the advice of a physician, either directly or indirectly. The intent of the author is only to offer information of a general nature to help you in your quest for emotional and spiritual well-being. In the event you use any of the information in this book for yourself, which is your constitutional right, the author and the publisher assume no responsibility for your actions.

Any people depicted in stock imagery provided by Getty Images are models, and such images are being used for illustrative purposes only. Certain stock imagery © Getty Images.

Scripture quotations marked KJV are from the Holy Bible, King James Version (Authorized Version). First published in 1611. Quoted from the KJV Classic Reference Bible, Copyright © 1983 by The Zondervan Corporation.

Print information available on the last page.

ISBN: 978-1-9822-7251-7 (sc)
ISBN: 978-1-9822-7252-4 (e)

Balboa Press rev. date: 08/19/2021

THIS BOOK IS DEDICATED TO:

I am deeply grateful for the Love and support of my husband Don, for his patience each time I was excited and wanted to read a portion of my writing that I had just completed. He listened intently, even though it is not a subject he is particularly drawn to and offered absolute delight for my excitement. He is the Love of my life for the past 28 years, and each day, I love him more. I am also grateful for each of my children, Christopher, Jonathan, and Alexis, who gave me the essential role in this lifetime: Mother. They have been a source of thousands more joyous and laughter-filled minutes than I can recall for every moment of tears of grief. Each of you has grown into the most caring and compassionate adults, and I am excited to see every step of your journey as you continue to discover yourselves and grow in your Love for the Divine spark within you.

Additionally, my soul tribes, the women who have been my rocks and my deep belly laughs, held me up when necessary and cheered me on to the finish line. My mother, Maureen, my sister, Colleen, my sister-in-laws Denise and Lisa, my Aunt Lynne and my cousin Miranda. My sisters from another mother, Pam, Melanie, Lyanna, Christine and Shannon. Lastly, the ones who helped shape my life but are no longer of this World, I feel your energy in everything I do, My Great-Grandmother May, Nana Wright, Nana Mckail and my Mother-in-Law Ellen. Each of you has made me who I am today; I hold a part of you in my heart forever.

CONTENTS

PART II: THE SEVEN GUARDIANS RELEASING OUR ATTACHMENTS TO THE EGO

April 24, 2020 – My Soul Speaks

There will be a great awakening. When we have completed the Earth's cleansing, humans will remember who they are – an expression of the Divine. Be still and come home. Listen from deep within your heart; this is where all the answers lie.

The Great Goddess is re-emerging, and with her, her King. When the two are reunited, the awakening will be complete. Every creature on Earth and beyond carry within their DNA the memory of the Creator/Creatrix and their Divine purpose on Earth. Listen to the Indigenous Tribes; they know, they hear. Their voices will help to guide us all back to what is essential. Honour the Earth, the Sky, the Moon, the Sun. Give great thanks to our Divine Mother/Father for breathing life into your incarnation at this time. Do not struggle; just be and enjoy every moment as it arises.

INTRODUCTION
– A SOFT WHISPER

The Divine Feminine is rising, being reconnected with her Beloved. During this deep cleansing of the Earth, humanity is awakening to our true nature – Love. It is all we are and all we can be. Yeshua instructed us that there are truly only these commandments we should live by, "And thou shalt love the Lord thy God with all thy heart, and with all thy soul, and with all thy mind, and with all thy strength: this is the first commandment."(King James Bible, Mark 12:30)[1] He added the second, which is equally important as the first: "And the second *is* like, *namely* this, Thou shalt love thy neighbour as thyself. There is none other commandment greater than these." (Mark 12:31)[2]. His true meaning was so profound and yet so misunderstood. We are each other; separation is an illusion. I am You, and You are me, and we are all part of one Divine Consciousness. When we love with all our hearts, we can look at all the Universe's intricacies and be content that all is well. This is a day-to-day practice. Even when we feel our prayers are not being answered or experiencing difficulties, our Love for our Creator never falters. Our souls are the innate part of us that, no matter what we are going through, knows that we are created by a power greater than ourselves when we sit in silence, and we can have a relationship directly with the Divine. With our minds means asking in every moment for divine guidance to lead us where we need to be, what we need to do

---

[1] Haynes, C. L., Jr, Haynes, C. L., Jr, Baker, L. L., & Danzey, E. (n.d.). *The Bible - Read and Study Free Online*. Bible Study Tools. Retrieved January 5, 2021, from https://www.biblestudytools.com/Mark 12:30
[2] Ibid. Mark 12:31

instead of relying on our understanding of what is necessary in each moment.

Loving with all our strength asks us to take this Love and put it into action in the World, to be in service to this incredible, immeasurable Love that is Infinite Love, our Creator. These commandments are interconnected; when we love ourselves and every living being, we honour our Divine Mother/Father as both masculine and Feminine and fulfill our purpose on this journey. We are energetic beings connected with the energy of the Universe, the planets, the animals, and one another, and we are all intimately connected to Infinite Love. In our human condition, we feel the need to name the sacred, unnameable, for us to comprehend this great Spirit of good. Love is the one word in our limited vocabulary that represents both the most incredible joy/bliss as well as our most significant grief. It is most often in our unspeakable suffering when we find the comfort and support of our ineffable Creator. There is something within us that cries out with yearning to know and feel this incredible Love to assure us that, in the words of Julian of Norwich, *'all shall be well, all shall be well, and all manner of things shall be well,'*[3]

As I begin writing, we are amid a global pandemic – COVID19. It is a time of deep hurt and deep healing, healing for us, our families, and most importantly, Mother Earth. Many of us are caught up in fear because we have not awakened our true selves. The protests of thousands against the stay-at-home orders are deeply connected with our ego and fear-based thinking. We are attached to the material World of greed, power, wealth, and physical matter. We have forgotten our true identities as co-creators, children of Divine Light, spiritual beings experiencing ourselves on this planet, and we have failed to love with all our hearts, souls, minds, and strength. A Course in Miracles lesson reminds us "To Be in the World, but not of it,"[4] our time here in this physical existence is temporary; do not attach yourself to it. Go inward and allow your Divine Self connected to Infinite Love to lead the way.

---

[3] Norwich, J. O. (2020). *Revelations of Divine Love by Julian of Norwich.* Independently published.

[4] Schucman, H (1992). *A Course in Miracles, Combined Volume: Text, Workbook for Students, Manual for Teachers, 2nd Edition* (2nd ed.). Foundation for Inner Peace.

PART 1
THE DIVINE FEMININE

CHAPTER 1

CHRISTIANITY: WHAT IS THE WHOLE STORY?

I FELT OUT OF PLACE FROM A YOUNG AGE; THE CHURCH WAS NOT A haven. My mother is a devout Roman Catholic, but I felt displaced. All the sitting, standing, and kneeling was far too conformed for me; a rebellion was stirring within me. At the age of fourteen, I became the first female altar server at the church we had attended since childhood. As I reflect, this was not because of my devotion or beliefs; it was to prove that a girl could do it, that we mattered to God (another word I am not comfortable using for its masculine connotations). This would become a pattern for me in my early adult life. At the age of fifteen, my job at McDonald's would see me fight for my rights to cook or even make french fries; jobs only boys were allowed to do. At sixteen, I often threatened to organize a union at Foodland because females were not permitted positions on the floor, only cashiers or behind the counters. This finally changed with the Employment Equity Act of 1986 to achieve equity in the workplace for minorities. Yes, the loophole at the time was that women were a minority in specific jobs!

All my life, I have been searching for my place—a woman's place in the church and the world. This search has led me down many paths and explorations. The most profound and surprising to me came through Yeshua (known as Jesus). I had denied him my entire life. I could not accept only one begotten Son of the Father. My mind and my soul screamed, "Where are the women? Why have my sisters and I been forgotten?"

In my dreams, both awake and asleep, she began to appear to me in visions and finally led me to her gospels, found in 1896. She was Yeshua's partner *(koinonos* in ancient Greek.) Jeans Yves Leloup, in his book *The Sacred Embrace of Jesus and Mary,* describes the translation of the term koinonos to "coupling and could be translated as 'fiancé,' 'companion' or spouse.'"[5] The one we refer to as Mary Magdalene is Miryam, Yeshua benJoseph's beloved bride. While Jesus reflects the archetype of the divine masculine Christ, Lord Christ, Mary Magdalene was the embodiment of the divine feminine Christ, Lady Christ. The gospel of Phillip tells us, "Three Women Named Mary: Three women always walked with the master: Mary his Mother, <his> sister, and Mary of Magdala, who is called his companion. For 'Mary' is the name of his sister, his Mother, and his companion."[6] Mary Magdalene is his sister of their shared divine mother/father, a term used often in the gnostic gospels; they greeted each other as brother or sister. She is also the mother of the disciples, a leader of the Nazarenes, and Yeshua's companion or beloved.

There are currently no texts that indicate their physical relationship, but we can surmise that theirs was a deep soul connection beyond the constraints of the physical realm. With the findings of the apocryphal gospels found at Nag Hammadi, specifically the gospels of Thomas and Phillip, along with her gospels, we see that Miryam was a beloved disciple who was part of Yeshua's close-knit circle.

Furthermore, as we will see as we progress through the chapters, she was his most advanced student, and she understood his earthly mission of leading us on the path of wholeness. I will use both names for each of these figures throughout the book—their original Hebrew names Yeshua and Miryam and their biblical names Jesus and Mary Magdalene—when quoting them from the different sources. Yeshua

---

[5] Leloup, J. (2006). *The Sacred Embrace of Jesus and Mary: The Sexual Mystery at the Heart of the Christian Tradition* (Translation ed.). Inner Traditions.

[6] Meyer, M. W., Pagels, E. H., Robinson, J. M., Funk, W., & Poirier, P. (2009). *The Nag Hammadi Scriptures: The Revised and Updated Translation of Sacred Gnostic Texts Complete in One Volume* (1st ed.). HarperOne.

and Miryam are the names their families and friends called them while alive. The "J" sound used to pronounce Jesus's name did not exist in Hebrew or Aramaic, and English in its current form did not exist even when writing the New Testament. In fact, according to several scholars, the Christian realist tells us, "In the original 1611 version of the King James Bible, the letter 'J' didn't exist in Hebrew. The original Hebrew name of Jesus is "Yhwshua," and that it took sixteen hundred years in the many translations for it to appear as Jesus in English."[7] (Winters, 2018)

Raymond W. Bernard, Ph.D., in his book *The Dead Sea Scrolls and the Life of the Original Christians: the Ancient Essenes,* explains that the discovery of the Dead Sea Scrolls at Qumran tells a very different early Christian story. I have read and studied many of the Nag Hammadi scriptures discovered but have yet to pursue these ancient Jewish and Hebrew texts. I will lean on Bernard for this information. Bernard argues that not one of the books found at Qumran mentions a saviour Man-God or a crucifixion. He states that the leader/teacher of the Essenes, the Greek Apollonius of Tyana, brought the teachings of Krishna, the Hindu deity, back to the neo-Pythagorean Jews at Qumran and translated them from Sanskrit to Aramaic; this became their gospel. These books of the Essenes speak of a teacher of righteousness, which Bernard states was Krishna, and these followers were considered Chrishn-ins. He states that Constantine combined the Western Sun God Iesus and the Eastern Chrishna to "create" Jesus Christ.

In the fourth century, while the council of Nicaea gathered with Emperor Constantine to formulate the new universal Roman religion, a Roman aristocrat and anti-Christian accused the priests of plagiary, stating that their Jesus and the writings were initially by Apollonius of Tyana. Apollonius was said to have lived simultaneously as Jesus and was a Greek Neopythagorean philosopher (Priaulx, 1860). He is reputed as a gentle man who loved all creatures.[8]

---

[7] Realist, V. A. P. B. T. C. (2018, April 8). *How did we get the name Jesus when the Letter "J" didn't exist in Jesus' time?* The Christian Realist. https://thechristianrealistcom. wordpress.com/2018/04/02/how-did-we-get-the-name-jesus-when-the-letter-j-didnt-exist-in-jesus-time/

[8] Priaulx, O., & de Beauvoir Priaulx, O. (2015). *The Indian Travels of Apollonius of Tyana.* Fb&c Limited.

I will not spend any more time researching any of this information; I introduce the hypothesis for further reading on your own. This raises our awareness that Christianity, the central religion of the masses, is not an entirely truthful rendition. The message is clear; we must continually seek the truth within ourselves and not rely on an outside authority whose aim was to control the masses. The Romans believed in a hierarchy, and their goal was to secure power for those they deemed worthy. The dispute at Nicaea debated whether "Jesus" was a man who ascended to God or God descended to earth in human form. The council established the Nicene Creed; only one father created all realms visible and invisible, and only one son of God. The creed also introduced that the Holy Spirit is masculine; even though spirit is a feminine word, an all-male trinity now enforced that the feminine was no longer anything of significance. She was removed entirely, delegated to a submissive servant to her superior males. The Nazarenes taught equality, not only with other humans but with the whole of the natural world; all creation belongs only to the Creator; therefore, we all belong equally.

Before the New Testament was a book, we know that these religious sects were persecuted for their beliefs. Whether these were Essenes, Nazarenes, neo-Pythagorean pagans, or early Christians, they taught and practiced a way of life that rendered all creatures equal. Many of the early teachings, recently discovered, spoke of an Earthly Mother and a Heavenly Father who were equally important and worthy of our reverence. The Essenes preached about forces or powers of both the visible material world and the invisible cosmic world surrounding us in every moment. Humans could pray, contemplate, and meditate upon these powers to absorb the energy into our consciousness. Their main messages were that the forces are within each of us and that in uniting our nature's masculine and feminine aspects within, we balance our world. The authority to believe or worship in any fashion is uniquely ours; only Spirit has authority over our souls. Direct communication with our souls and Spirit is what is needed to be restored in our hearts and communities. It is suspicious that as soon as the Nicene Council integrated the new Roman religion, all other writings that contradicted orthodox beliefs were burned or buried deep in the deserts to be protected from the plunder.

As I began my search for the lost feminine more intensely in 2017 after a major crisis in our lives forced me to stop working for a few months and go inward, I realized that she had been calling to me my entire life. I started to inquire from the many Christians I knew who could recite every word in the Bible where the feminine was; they would show me many prominent women. No matter how many great acts they had performed, the ones they cited were always still sidekicks to the more powerful masculine. I wanted the Goddess partner to God, not a subservient, lesser female who only plays a supporting role, and I liked the lead! It is my deep belief that Yeshua and Miryam came to Earth together to share the Good News that "God" as we know or as portrayed as a "Father" is a misnomer. The Creator of all is infinite light and genderless, and the image or likeness humanity describes is our soul, not our physical stature as the church fathers would have us believe. Our souls are pure light and love, the most authentic image of our likeness to our Creator and the cosmic cycles of creativity, and a unified dance of the energy polarities of masculine and feminine forces. In the creation story in the Bible, we read, "And God said, 'Let there be light: and there was light.'"[9] (Genesis 1:3) We are the light, and our soul's purpose is to shine our light in the universe.

I believe it is time for Miryam to rise from her hidden cave, next to her beloved companion Yeshua, so both become partners and equals as Sons and Daughters of a great Mother/Father Creator/Creatrix. We have witnessed our world over the last 4,000 years under patriarchal, misogynist domination, war, famine, inequality, and racism. The coronavirus has shined a blaring light on many of these injustices. If the feminine aspect of God taught through Yeshua and Miryam's ministry as sacred partners had not been edited, redacted, or in some cases completely removed, our world these past 2,000 years would look very different today. The feminine side of all of us (male and female) reflects nurturing, kindness, and compassion, and a balance of masculine and feminine must return to our hearts for the entire world to heal.

The silencing of the feminine has led to our Mother Earth suffering

---

[9] Haynes, C. L., Jr, Haynes, C. L., Jr, Baker, L. L., & Danzey, E. (n.d.). *The Bible - Read and Study Free Online.* Bible Study Tools. Retrieved January 5, 2021, from https://www.biblestudytools.com/Genesis 1:3 KJV

almost irreparable damage, so much destruction under a masculine-dominated society. Masculine and feminine are again not relating to our physical incarnations; these are traits that each of us carries within our DNA, the yin and yang of Eastern traditions. We have been living in an imbalanced world for far too long. It is time for humanity to awaken and to come back to our true identity as limitless, eternal beings—as children of love. It is time for a deep cleanse of our political and socioeconomic structures that stifle our growth and true potential as cocreators. Awaken our dreams and deepest soul desires. The old systems are crumbling to open us to something even more significant than we can imagine. Miracles are being witnessed all around the Globe as communities come together to offer each other support. As more of us awaken and embrace the Bride and Bridegroom, we will begin to be rooted in the Feminine (creative) and the masculine (producer) and the entire planet will live in abundance. When we balance both, we experience generosity, cooperation, and a world in balance, where there is plenty for every living being and creature.

I spent two hours in deep meditation, choosing Yeshua as my mentor for a deepening exercise taught to me in Mirabai Starr's book Wild Mercy. I felt the Divine presence as though he was physically sitting with me as I poured out my soul. I gave over all my fears, concerns and failures directly to him. I sincerely felt his calm and peace embrace me, allowing me to be completely open and vulnerable and expose my deepest soul desires. When I finally had emptied my soul, I felt a warm breeze and realized my face was soaked with tears. I gently opened my eyes and felt a deep sense of peace come over me. As I looked into the sky, the clouds appeared as Angel wings, and a blue orb appeared. I was overcome with the knowledge that the presence of this beautiful master wisdom teacher had indeed been with me. I looked over at the tree and another sign; branches had twisted into the shape of the Christian symbol for Jesus, the fish. The following day, as I headed for the shower, a soft voice whispered to me, "The Seven Guardians." I stood wrapped in my towel and looked around the room; was this my mind/imagination? Or as in the Gospels of Mary, the nous, the place Yeshua describes as between the Soul & Spirit; the eye of the heart that can perceive the Divine from inside ourselves? The Seven Guardians continued to echo within me throughout the day, and I recalled a book I had read the previous year by Jehanne De Quillan that had indeed spoken to me, "The Gospel of the Beloved Companion, The complete Gospels of Mary Magdalene." As I frantically searched my shelves for this book, my husband questioned the importance of finding it. Twenty-seven years of living with me, he does not often ask about the voices I hear and tends to appreciate that eventually, more profound answers come to me in kairos or perfect Divine timing. As soon as I held the book in my hands again, a deep knowing came over me. I turned to my husband and explained that I was being led to write about this. I had no idea what my writing would lead to or why this book, in particular, was of supreme importance. Still, I knew the answers lay inside the covers of this Gospel that had awakened my soul. I did not question how or why, but I knew deeply that this was a message I had to study deeper. Even as I began writing this morning, I meditated and asked again if I was on the right path? The Divine Feminine card I pulled from my Meggan Watterson deck was, of course, Mary Magdalene. My yard has been filled with a party of Blue Jays all day – messengers from the other realm to remind us to persevere, communicate our truths. Heaven always speaks to us; the sacred within us must be opened to listening. The Goddess reawakened a passion within me that I had no idea had been lying dormant. My soul was no longer willing to be kept quiet and subdued. I was ready to speak from my soul with all her authenticity and power. My husband has reminded me there will be pushback; many Christians I know warn that many of the books found at Qumran and Nag Hammadi are false prophets. I believe we are at a pivotal moment in our existence, where we can no longer remain ignorant. These books were found when humanity was ready to understand Yeshua and Miryam's actual messages, not edited versions by men who gained a lot of power and wealth by leading the people astray.

As my more profound journey has continued and my research of the Divine lost Feminine, I learned the Fish was a symbol much older than Christianity and Jesus. The fish is an ancient yoni symbol – a yoni womb fish; derived from the Vesica Pisces in sacred geometry to represent the female vulva. "There are various meanings ascribed the Vesica Pisces, which is the intersection of two, overlapping spheres; such as the union of heaven and Earth in the body of Christ, the root element of the Flower of Life, the merging of God and Goddess, the vagina of the female goddess, the first pattern at the basis of all trigonometric configurations, square roots and harmonic dimensions; a source of great power and vitality, and as an overlying template that intersects with all the points on the Tree of Life. The Tree of Life, Flower of Life, and the Seed of Life overlap perfectly, with the Vesica Pisces providing all of the elements of the Flower of Life and all the coordinates for the Tree of Life."[10] Baptism rites also date much farther back than John the Baptist, and initiates were often passed through a giant yoni, a sign of rebirth or born again. Yeshua was a lover of the goddess, and his message included her. It is my deepest hope that humanity will grow to honour her once again, and we will all rejoice when the Bride and Bridegroom are reunited in our hearts.

Once I began on this journey, there was no returning for me. It was a feeling of complete knowing the truth. In the beginning, I felt so angry and frustrated from the lies and betrayal of the past few thousand years by the Church. The blatant and often forceful silencing of our Creator's Feminine aspect wanted to scream from the rooftop! The Crusades, Inquisition, Witch hunts ripped me apart. The apocryphal gospels, specifically The Gospel of Mary, invited me to learn an entirely different Christian story. As previously discussed, and although it is still not clear in the writings, it is in my heart that Yeshua and Miryam's message and example of living was a divine sacred union of the masculine and Feminine.

In the Gospels of Phillip; Chapter 24, Saying 22 Yeshua says, "When you make the two into one, and when you make the inner as the outer, and the upper as the lower, and when you make the male and female into a single one so that the male shall not be male, and the female shall not be female … then you will enter the kingdom."[11] This

---

[10] How The Vesica Pisces Explains Creation And The Arrow Of Time | Science of Wholeness Is Your Highest Fulfillment. Scienceofwholeness.com. Wordpress (Last accessed 2021)

[11] Meyer, M. W., Pagels, E. H., Robinson, J. M., Funk, W., & Poirier, P. (2009). *The Nag Hammadi Scriptures: The Revised and Updated Translation of Sacred Gnostic Texts Complete in One Volume* (1st ed.). HarperOne. (*Gospel of Philip 59:6-10*).

message is a call to remember we are not of this Earth; the physical bodies we represent in our short time here are vessels that carry our higher selves. Our higher selves, our souls, are genderless. This saying from Phillip's Gospel is inviting us to detach from any previous beliefs or limiting ideas. To enter the kingdom within us, our souls, we must release everything taught about attachments on the physical realm, release any expectations or outcomes and surrender to Divine will. Now is our opportunity to experience life as a Fully Human and Fully Divine realization. Sacred sexual union with a partner is a deep knowing that the two have to be united to become the whole. Our grand creator/creatrix; is a beautiful harmony of both the feminine and masculine aspects; this saying reminds us we need a balance of both. The Feminine has been silenced for too long. Every creature on this planet is a reflection of the imagination of our creation.

As we imagine, we create. If we collectively imagine a world of peace, harmony, joy and love, we can make it. Yeshua said, "Once you realize who you are, you will do greater things than me. When you say Mountain move, it will move."[12] Now is the time of great remembering, a time to live our authentic true selves, that of co-creators! We are here to adore and cherish the Love within each of us and every living creature. We have become so separated from our true essence and have come to cherish the World of form. We idolize our cars, houses, jobs, money; while all of these are wonderful and allow us to enjoy life, they are all temporary. We must ask ourselves, "Who am I if any of these are taken away?" The true you lies much deeper and is eternal; put your energy and focus on building that relationship.

The Churches of the past 2,500 years are becoming obsolete. Humanity is beginning to awaken to their souls and our connection with all of creation. The patriarchal churches created a God in the image of a male human; a father figure, the complete opposite is true, our eternal; genderless souls are the Infinite Spirit's image, the Creator of all. Our souls are formless, lasting, and free from physical form limits. We must now ask ourselves the more profound questions; how can we catalyze change from a place of transcendental love? How can we

---

[12] Ibid. (Gospel of Thomas pp. 152, saying 106).

9

integrate our highest self with our primal needs, unite our humanity with our divinity, transform the dense matter into infinite love? Yeshua and Miryam left us a blueprint, a path to realizing our soul's purpose of having direct communication with Infinite Light. Miryam has given us a higher knowledge, knowledge of the heart; she calls us into the fifth dimension, the higher realms of existence of non-duality. The Divine Feminine is an energy that transcends time and space and is now ready to enter into the collective consciousness.

This book began to be created from journal entries for over a year, research, study, intimate communication through deep meditation and daily spiritual practices. I wasn't quite sure at the time what it was becoming. Upon completing the third or fourth draft, I finally accepted it as a book I wanted to publish and share. Although my authentic voice has been silenced for most of my life, my thoughts on the inequities in the church and a soul belief in a higher power who is both masculine and feminine are unable to stay quiet. I am deeply grateful to the many scholars and theologians who have spent years translating these newly discovered gospels that provide insight into perhaps the earliest Christians, or Nazarenes, as they would have been called. Unfortunately, The Gospel of the Beloved Companion has not been authenticated, and the original texts are missing. We will explore the guardians of the ego as they were presented to Miryam in a vision of Yeshua in her heart from these writings. I do believe these are the words of Miryam, and regardless of their validity, they present us with an opportunity to live a more peaceful life in joy, acceptance and equality. I advise anyone who reads this book to read The Gospel of the Beloved Companion, The Complete Gospel of Mary; there are profoundly moving passages where you will be able to hear the voice of Miryam. Additionally, I will show verses from the translated Gospel of Mary found in the desert and other gospels to support the text and give a clearer picture of this incredible disciple Miryam.

My Soul Speaks

Trust that every moment is perfect; everything is unfolding in the exact optimum way. Say yes to everything. Invite triggers; everyone who triggers you is your teacher; they allow your soul to grow and evolve. Be at peace with whatever shows up. Each moment is guiding me to the highest Infinite possibility. Do not attach to the outcome; follow your intuition. If something that appears to be negative shows up, ask where I am not following my path; where do I need to realign? Whether a positive or negative appearing event or person arrives in your life, practice gratitude, be thankful for the lesson.

Exercise

Sit comfortably and close your eyes; breathe into your heart. Imagine a ministry led by Yeshua and Miryam, embraced by all, a fellowship of equality.

We cannot change the past, but we can change from this day forward. Enter into your heart and envision a world where we respect and care for every living creature. Send healing prayers to Mother Gaia, the Earth waters, the sky and the living creatures residing in each of these. Our prayers are powerful and can create immediate healing.

If you feel called to, create a prayer group within your circle of friends or family and meet virtually at least once a week. Enter into this space together and send healing prayers as a unified group. We are stronger together!

Affirmation – A Healing Prayer

Dear Spirit, our living Mother, our Heavenly Father, guide me in everything I think, say and do for the greatest good of all creation. May my every contribution in this physical existence reflect only your will. Help me to hear the calling of my soul, my deepest connection to you; my angel guides and ascended masters to create a world where only love reigns. Guide me to the people, places, and things to share this love and assist in healing our planet. Let me shine my light so others will feel empowered to let their light shine.

CHAPTER 2

PAST LIFE - TABITHA

I ONCE VISITED A MEDIUM AND CHANNELER; IN HER READING, SHE told me gazelles surrounded me, their long manes represented my hair, and she stated that they were a symbol of graceful beauty. She continued to explain that they were bowing down to me; they honoured me. The message was that in unity, we are stronger. A few months later, I had a vision; it appeared as though it was my wedding day long ago. My gown was reminiscent of the Egyptian women's attire centuries ago, white, with gold shoulder straps and a golden sash around my waist. The skies were an incredible blue, sunbeams were shining down on me and warming my dark skin, and the air was buzzing with excitement. It felt similar to what I imagined were Mayday or Beltane celebrations of the early centuries, a celebration of masculine and feminine, men and women's joining. I had long, flowing, deep auburn hair beyond my waist, and my husband-to-be was a large, burly, jovial man of great importance.

As the vision continued, I could see our home, a great fortress, where we had enjoyed many wonderful years together, with a large community of faithful, loving brothers and sisters who celebrated their mutual Divine parentage. I seemed to be constantly surrounded by many children, and people from all over came to me to heal illnesses. Suddenly, the vision grew very dark; I felt a heaviness in my centre, as though I was a seer looking into our future at that time. I warned my husband of dark forces coming to our village when instantly, the skies went dark, and the heavens opened up with pouring rains and strong winds. I felt my heart ripped out as I realized my husband had been murdered, and I had fled with my women and children to an underground cave beneath a well. We had been forcefully removed from our homes and had become a community of women, priestesses; with our children to care for alone, all our men had been slaughtered. As we sat around a fire, I can sense that I am highly regarded as a healer and seer. Throughout the vision, the name associated with my person was Tabitha; this name echoed continually. As I slowly re-entered my body to come back to the present moment, the name Tabitha stayed with me, as did the sadness of the brutal invasion. I immediately gathered my pen and journal and wrote down everything I had remembered.

I then phoned my dear friend Christine, one friend who does not question my visions or think I am crazy when I share them with her. The name Tabitha did not resonate with either of our memories as a prominent figure in any historical or religious accounts. In researching the name, starting with the Bible, I found that Tabitha in Aramaic means gazelle; I was intrigued to learn more. Additionally, the name Tabitha translated to Greek is Dorcas, which means deer or doe and a symbol of graceful beauty. What? My mind was reeling; these were not mere coincidence; the medium predictions and this vision happened months apart. I had to find the CD recording of the reading and verify these enormous synchronicities.

In my current incarnation, I am often visited by a family of deer in my yard and have always had a very spiritual connection with them. When they arrive and turn to me, I thank them for the reminder to seek a deeper meaning and meditate immediately following the interaction. As my research deepened, I discovered that Tabitha had been a great disciple of Yeshua, possibly even a priestess of Miryam. She is referenced in Acts of the Apostles (9:36-42). Wikipedia says this about the disciple Tabitha; "Acts recounts that when she died, she was mourned by "all the widows ... crying and showing (Peter) the robes and other clothing that she had made while she was still with them" (Acts 9:39). The Greek construct used in this passage indicates that the widows were the recipients of her charity, but she may also have been a widow herself. She was likely a woman of some means, given her ability to help the poor. "The disciples present called upon Peter, who

14

came from nearby Lydda to the place where her body was being laid out for burial, and raised her from the dead."[13] In all her sentiments, she is described as a gentle woman who cared deeply for her community, with unconditional Love. The fact that she is described as a widow, who helped other widows, confirmed my vision of the village's men killed in some attack. For the past few days, following the full moon eclipse, I have felt an incredible pressure in my solar plexus; I have cried out of the blue, driving in my car, walking, anywhere, anytime, without prompting. I found myself on my knees in surrender, begging for a sign of my purpose in life, questioning this book and whether it deserved to be published and shared, a prevalent theme the entire time writing this. This morning, when looking for something in my car, I found four pages that had ripped out of my journal, and for some reason, were torn and folded. The pages were the above-described encounter; thank you, Divine Mother/Father, you always answer my prayers. In an instant, I found the journal entry and listened again and again to the reading. Combining these with factual evidence that matched the Tabitha in the bible, I encountered firsthand knowledge of my purpose in this incarnation. In my most profound memory, hidden in my subconscious, is the realization that I had walked beside these great teachers, Yeshua and Miryam, in one of my lifetimes. I knew their story intimately; I had to remember it, bring it forward into this lifetime, and share its truth with the world.

Once again, evidence of our interconnectedness, we ebb and flow between the portals of form and formlessness. The cycle of birth-death-rebirth continues over and over again. Most people living today have forgotten their ability to access psychic forces, speak with the Spirit realms, visit their past lives, or connect directly with the Divine. This innate ability is awakening in many around the World; our evolution to the fifth-dimensional reality is imminent. I have experienced visions my entire life in this incarnation, whether it was visited by loved ones who had passed over or messages of a divine kind. These visions were not something I shared outside a very close circle; the Western World has not been open or accepting of this very feminine way of listening

---

[13] Syswerda, J. E. (2018). *Women of the Bible: 52 Bible Studies for Individuals and Groups*. HarperChristian Resources.

for guidance from within. The male disciples taught more of a way to live by rules and act as Jesus would act. That Miryam saw her beloved Rabbouni in a vision within her heart was a validation of epic proportions for me.

Having inner vision since childhood and not being believed or labelled as over-imaginative, I felt euphoria like never before; Mary's Gospel confirmed I was not crazy, nor experiencing hallucinations. The imaginal realms are just as natural as the physical World of matter, the word imaginal in this sense is a term first coined by Henry Corbin in his paper "Mundas Imaginalis or the Imaginary and the Imaginal." Mary asks, "Lord, I see you now in this vision." And the Lord answered: "You are blessed, for the sight of me does not disturb you."[14](Mary 10:12-15.) Mary is not describing a realm of imagination or illusion; this vision is where the soul recognizes more than just our one-dimensional reality. It is between the invisible worlds of multi-dimensionality and the visual material we view with only our five senses. I have been asked how I access transcendental visions, and I can honestly answer I do not have a firm answer. Is it a practiced state? A natural state – born with our psychic abilities more open? Or is it in believing, having an open heart and faith in the grace of the Divine? For myself, I think it is possibly a combination of all of the above. Mary continues, "Lord, when someone meets you in a moment of vision, is it through the soul (psyche) that they see, or is it through the Spirit (Pneuma)" The Teacher answered: "It is neither through the soul nor the spirit, but the nous between the two which sees the vision, and it is this which (…)"[15] (Mary 10:18-25). The following pages are missing from the original papyrus in all three copies discovered, pages 11-14. The nous, translated from Greek to English, is mind; this is not the mind as we know it today, intellect; it was in Yeshua and Miryam's time, more associated with intuition, connected with the cosmic mind. Meggan Watterson describes it as a bridge between our physical body and Spirit, much as Christianity would call the Holy Spirit.

As Joan of Arc exclaimed, "I am not afraid; I was born to do this!"

---

[14] Leloup, J., Rowe, J., & Needleman, J. (2002). *The Gospel of Mary Magdalene* (First Paperback Edition). Inner Traditions.(page 31)

[15] Ibid. (page 31)

CHAPTER 3

THE HEART BRAIN

SCIENTISTS ARE NOW DISCOVERING THAT THE HEART IS COMPOSED of an intricate network of neurotransmitters, complex ganglia, proteins and support cells, a replica of the brain in the head.[16] The heart-brain sends signals to the head brain tied to emotion, how to feel throughout the body in certain circumstances. The head brain is logical, opinionated, judgmental, filled with fears and rules (ego). Our authentic selves' heart-brain functions higher emotions, such as Love, compassion and our I AM presence and guides our intuitive thoughts (soul).

In January 2006, my father, who had been battling liver disease for many years, was in the final few weeks of his incarnation in this lifetime. As the organs began shutting down, his doctor came to our home, where we were caring for him. As the doctor was leaving, he handed my mother my father's death certificate. He explained it would not be long now, and there was no need for him to come back; the nurse could add the actual day and time of death when it arrived. The immediate cause of death was heart failure. In my naivety, I was perplexed and asked him how he would know the final cause of death. His response was, "It is eventually what everyone dies from because it is only when the heart stops beating, no pulse are you officially declared dead." I have pondered this response often over the years. As I began practicing meditation by shifting my awareness into my heart, I knew that my heart chakra, the centre of my being, is where my soul resides;

---

[16] HeartMath Institute. (2020, December 20). *Science of the Heart.* https://www.heartmath.org/research/science-of-the-heart/

it is the centre of my I AM presence, my eternal self. When our soul leaves this physical body, it no longer keeps the heart pumping.

My Father's final moments as a human on this Earth realm were beautiful. It was incredibly peaceful with his family all gathered for days. His dearest friends were able to say their goodbyes. In his final three days in a coma state, reserving all of his energy for the arduous journey back through his Divine Mother's womb, my earth mother whispered all of their beautiful memories, sang their favourite songs and held him. His children, brother, and sister-in-law spoke to him gently and thanked him for his life here. In his final moments, his eyes opened, and he looked directly at each one of us. My eldest brother Danny was upstairs, and as my mother yelled to him to get downstairs, my father's eyes darted around the room, and I recognized fear. It was not the fear of dying; it was the fear of not seeing his firstborn for the last time. Danny arrived at the bottom of the bed, and my father held his gaze and took his final breath. I watched as the light disappeared; my father had the most stunning clear sky-blue eyes; upon death, the colour left, and only grey eyes stared.

Many believe that when a person dies and their eyes open, they are afraid or unsure about their next world journey. My Father did not subscribe to any belief system, but he and I had many conversations about the next part of our journey when this incarnation comes to a close during his lengthy illness. I learned quickly that he was tired of the question, "How are you?" He was sick, and he was dying. Instead, I asked, "What are you feeling today? What reflections of this life have you been contemplating?" It would spark many deeply spiritual conversations. I have been visited by people who have travelled the journey from physical incarnation to the realm of no body since I was a child. The visits never alarmed me because there was peace emanating from their energy in my visions, every one of the visits was a reassurance that they had made it to the other side and were ok. These were the conversations my father and I had in his final months, and he would often stare quietly and then ask me if I believed this to be true. I made him promise to let me know when he arrived in any way that felt right to his soul. I think he was afraid because he was unsure what was next. Still, these conversations gave him optimism; death was inevitable, how we face it is a final testament to our character during this lifetime. It has been scientifically proven; we are made up of energy with no beginning and no end; energy does not dissolve; it just exists elsewhere. I spent many years hiding my abilities as a death whisperer because the adults in my life informed me that I had imagined these visits, or the signs that the loved one had sent me could have happened to anyone, and quite frankly, it freaked people out. I did not cry for weeks after my father's passing, and I called his cell phone number every day to hear his voicemail, which sadly was just his abrupt first and last name. A few weeks after his physical death, I knelt at his gravestone and cried uncontrollably.

I was living in fear of a financial crisis, my husband had lost his six-figure income and jobs in his field were not in abundance. I told my dad how afraid I was when a gentle breeze lifted my hair. I closed my eyes and looked up into the sky to feel the coolness on my cheeks. When I reopened my eyes and looked down, the breeze had carried the corner of an American $1,000.00 bill. The only piece of the money left was the front corner with the rare amount (these large bills have not been in circulation for eons) and on the back that read "In God we trust." I took three deep breaths, laughed and thanked him for his message of hope and reminding me with a tangible sign that his energy was near me. His soul was eager to inform me that I can feel his Spirit even though I cannot see his body. The corner of the bill is safely stored in a zip lock bag and hangs on my fridge to remind me that the invisible realms are within reach and are genuine.

The soul directs and guides the heart-brain, in my opinion. As the fetus's heart begins to beat at 22 days, this is when the soul starts its experience as an incarnated human and Spiritual Guide. Science has been unable to discover how the heart begins beating, keeps it going, or even controls its rhythm. Perhaps it is not a question for modern materialistic science. It is an opportunity for us to remember who we are, children of intricate, complex Creators, A Divine Mother/Father. If we live in awe and reverence for the divinity in our human creation, listen more to our heart-brain than our head-brain, we will gain greater clarity, peace and a deeply intuitive knowing of every next move for the greatest good of all. We all have life force energy surging within us; a web of interconnectedness binds us and all of creation together within this energy. How will you choose to use this powerful energy to co-create with Infinite Source? We have the power of choice (free will) to create from our life force energy for the highest good of all creation; we are the warriors of light who can be a catalyst of change for the World.

I have recently begun to study translations of the ancient Aramaic language of Miryam and Yeshua, the language they spoke with one another and used in their teachings. Interestingly, Aramaic is a language with many interpretations of every word. When the original writings were translated to Greek, then Latin and eventually modern English, they lost their "heart" meaning, their spiritual meaning. Aramaic, like its current form Arabic, is a language with several tiers of importance; when one speaks these languages, we interpret based on more than just the words. We listen to the tone, the body language and the universal mystical meaning. Mysticism was deemed heretical in the early centuries of the Roman Church, and yet, Jesus, with whom they based their teachings, was a middle Eastern mystic. Through prayer and meditation, Yeshua and Miryam received their guidance through direct communication with the divine. Later mystics would be charged, tried and often murdered for admitting, Joan of Arc and Marguerite Porette, along with many others, had experienced direct communication with the divine and executed for it.

When Yeshua and Miryam taught, the listeners would not just "hear" the words; the messages would resonate within their bodies, they would feel the meaning. As I recalled a My soul speaks, which I have added to this book, it was a revelation for me when I heard the words in a vision that it was not the words that were important, but the message. The words are not essential; how do you feel when you read or hear certain words? This is an individual journey, and each of us will feel and perceive differently from another. This is what was meant by the "ears to hear, or the eyes to see." With our inner vision, the divine speaks our language, and it is only within the heart-brain that we can comprehend their spiritual meaning. Many of the male disciples wanted Yeshua to provide them with all the answers; his messages were incomprehensible to their head-brain thinking. Still, he continually reminded them, they had to do the work from within, and all would be revealed.

Miryam was a conscientious student; her only focus was on the queendom both within and among us. She rigorously practiced her spiritual rituals to uncover the deeper, more profound meaning of her human life. Yeshua spoke in a transformative language with several purposes; through contemplation with our inner vision, the words' hidden meaning is revealed to the student willing to hear the mystical translation related to the divine, the cosmos, and the universe. Western society has lost this powerful way to interpret from within and the more profound unitive language, the Galilean Aramaic of Yeshua and Miryam. We interpret everything "literally" instead of figuratively; we leave no room for interpretation. In the following few chapters, we will discuss the revelation that opened my heart to a much more powerful message that the Masters Yeshua and Miryam taught us. I ask you to keep an open heart and allow whatever messages resonate with you. Allow your inner heart-brain to interpret what vibrates in your body, do not pay too much attention to the words; these are my perceptions. Feel for yourself what these messages may be revealing to you; how do they make you feel? What is true for you, and what changes will you make in your own life to match any new vibrations? Imagine what our society would be like today if the church and governments had not silenced the feminine aspect of our Creator and ourselves.

> "If we take something to be the truth, we may cling to it so much that when the truth comes and knocks at our door, we won't want to let it in." Thich Nhat Hanh

My Soul Speaks

There is a reason broken souls, especially women, are drawn to you. Share the beauty of the morning with them, the moments you take in the sunrise, to be grateful and appreciate the abundance and beauty in nature. It is not your job to fix them, by sharing your joy and peace will help them find theirs. I gently close my eyes, a soft smile touching my lips, just listening to the sounds, the vast array of birdsong, the wind rustling the bountiful leaves, the pitter-patter of rain on the gazebo. One bird in the distance sings a song that sounds like she is repeating, "Thank you, Thank you, Thank you." I sway with her music, my hand over my heart and sing with her, thank you, Divine Mother/Father; we are grateful for the opportunity to be living this blessed life.

Affirmation

I rise with the Sun and welcome each new day with awe, and I have no expectations. I know that the Divine has a plan for me, and I follow my inner guidance to where I am led.

Exercise

- Have a pen and journal with you to write down any messages or insights that come to you through this exercise.
- Sit or lie comfortably; close your eyes and take three deep breaths; in through the nose and out through the mouth.
- Focus on your inner vision and move your attention to your heart centre (between your breasts in the centre of your chest).
- Feel your in-breath filling your heart centre with Love and light, and your out-breath releasing any tension or negative feelings. Once you feel connected, breathe normally and ask your soul what it wants you to know your inner guidance. Listen deeply; some of what you hear may not make sense immediately. When you are ready, open your eyes and journal for at least ten full minutes. Do not stop to edit or correct, just free-flow writing.

What messages was your soul communicating with you? The answers may not come right away but continue to do this exercise regularly. Often, I have returned to my old journals six months, a year or even longer, and all of a sudden, the words and messages resonate with me. All is revealed in Divine timing when we are ready. Have faith, trust and patience.

CHAPTER 4

THE CHAKRA ENERGY SYSTEM

I WILL BRIEFLY EXPLAIN THE ASSOCIATED CHAKRA AND A SHORT description of their relevance to the lesson at each bough. The chakras are an energy network system that bridges the physical and spiritual forms of existence. These central energy centres run up the spine and create a connection with our physical body and spiritual body. The seven colours of the rainbow are the same ones reflected within each Chakra and are also the seven steps of a spiritual path, another indication of the Universe's oneness. They are described in Mary's Gospels' authenticated copies as the seven powers of the ego and The Gospel of the Beloved Companion as the Seven Guardians. The number seven continually appears as a spiritual number throughout time and is often a spiritual transformation path. The lower chakras connect us with the Earth and bodily desires. In contrast, the upper chakras connect us with the Divine and our spiritual nature, with the heart being the centre, the bridge that unites the two.

The Chakras take in and emanate energy from the Universal life force to keep us functioning at optimal levels. We are both a spiritual energy body and the subtle body and a physical body. I believe Yeshua's missing years were spent travelling and training with some of the most advanced spiritual advisers in many Eastern traditions, and one of those would have been in India. In Indian heritage, the chakras have been called the seven shining places in the body. Known as the brain (Sahasrara - the door to God), medulla oblongata (Ajna - eye of intuition), and five spinal centers—cervical (Visuddha - especially pure), dorsal (Anahata - unhurt or unstuck; beyond the hurt lies a spiritual place where no hurt exists), lumbar (Manipura lustrous gem), sacral (Svadhisthana - the dwelling place of the self), and coccygeal (Muladhara - root of existence)— through which the Spirit becomes connected. Each colour emanates a vibrational frequency, and this frequency increases as you move up the chakras. Each chakra is also associated with our emotions; when our energy moves downward, we are stuck in negative energies like anger, hatred, and greed. When our energy moves upward, we emit positive energy such as love and compassion; we are evolving our awareness and Consciousness. The title given to Yeshua was Christ, referring to Christ consciousness, the highest state of Consciousness that one can attain, wholly immersed in Spirit's presence within and all around. With a balanced energy system, we flow easily with divine knowledge, and as children of the Divine Source of all creation, we all can attain Christ's Consciousness while embodied in the physical realm.

The importance of understanding the chakras is vital to all of humanity. Scientific evidence proves we are so much more than our physical body; within the chakra system is the core of who we are as human spiritual beings. Ultimately, we are musical beings; light, sound, colour, frequency, chakras, and consciousness must align for our instruments to live at optimal levels both physically and spiritually. If our root chakra is not grounded, we live too much in the clouds and have a disconnection to the Earth; if it is too grounded, we are too attached to the material World. We need to work on each chakra for balance through meditation, mantras, music. I feel that this information is relevant to the inner teachings of Miryam. It is not only the physical body that is covered when we follow her guidance and way to the heart; it is, more importantly, our spiritual beings that are healed and balanced. Energetic vibrations of emotions resonate with the energy centre closest to it; this is why low vibrational emotions like anger, guilt and shame can lead to disease in the liver; reproductive organs and colon.

On the other hand, love, Joy, Peace and enlightenment vibrate at 500+ THz and create harmony within the physical body. As Spirit beings on Earth and material beings with souls, we must focus on the evolution of both to be in balance. While the physical body is temporary and the soul is eternal, it is essential to focus on both while embodied to do the Good's work while we are here.

> "Every thought and experience you've ever had in your life gets filtered through these chakra databases. Each event is recorded into your cells ... in effect, your biography becomes your biology."[17] Caroline Myss

[17] Myss, C. (1996). *Anatomy of the Spirit: The Seven Stages of Power and Healing* (1st ed.). Harmony.

CHAPTER 5

The Gospel of Mary Magdalene and The Gospel of the Beloved Companion, The Complete Gospels of Mary

The Gospels of Mary, discovered in 1896 in Upper Egypt and later fragments from two Greek editions, were apparently in reasonably good shape when found and finally translated. The exception is that all three copies found are missing the same pages: 1 through 6 and 11 through 14. The manuscript begins on page 7 in the middle of a passage. This Gospel is radically different from the New Testament Gospels, in which many correctors were hired to edit and redact the teachings. The Gospel of Mary provides us with a deeper understanding of Yeshua's teachings that Spiritual development begins from within and a clearer picture of the state of Consciousness Miryam had achieved. As many of us know, history is written by the victors. Romans edited the canonical gospels to attract and eventually enforce brutally Roman pagans to one universal belief system. Many of Yeshua's teachings are captured in these gospels, but they have been severely edited and misinterpreted in the translations. This is the only Gospel we currently have written by a female disciple, further proof that the teachings were shared equally among both male and female followers of Yeshua.

No authority, other than the good (no mention of a Father God in this Gospel), is responsible for our spiritual enlightenment. Perhaps

Yeshua refers to the heart-brain — focus here, and all the answers are available to us, the part of ourselves that remembers who we are. If we listen closely, all the answers are within; the Kingdom of Heaven resides in us and is in our midst. The only sin is believing that this material world is our home and immersed in the illusion that we are only a body. When translated from the Greek hamartanó, the word sin means to err, be mistaken; lastly, to miss or wander from the path of uprightness and honour, to do or go wrong.[18] In fact, in the Gospel of Mary, Peter asks Yeshua what the sin of the World is and "The Teacher answered: 'There is no sin. It is you who make sin exist, when you act according to the habits of your corrupted nature, this is where sin lies.'"[19] (Mary 7:15-19). Our corrupted nature is the ego out of balance, in control of our actions. The child of the living Spirit (Anthropos) is 100% Human and 100% Divine; we are both of these at all times, the ego and the soul. "Anthropos' as a part of an expression in the original Greek New Testament is translated as Son of man."[20] Jesus was referenced as the Son of man in the gnostic gospels, a fully integrated human; the Romans later changed this to the Son of God. It is only in over-identifying with the ego that we are out of balance in our energy centres, physical manifestations and spiritual health. When we allow one of the ego's guardians to control us, we are trapped in our physical existence's linear/chronological structure when we are not aware or conscious. Only when we raise our Consciousness, be aware each time the ego leads us and drop back into the nous, the eye of the heart, for guidance to make rational decisions in partnership with our divinity. The nous is our opportunity to perceive the soul and repeatedly resurrect while embodied in this incarnation. It is where we have visions and communicate with the Spiritual realms while we are a body.

---

[18] Contributors to Wikimedia projects. (2020, December 28). *Anthropos*. Wikipedia. https://en.wikipedia.org/wiki/hamartanó

[19] Leloup, J., Rowe, J., & Needleman, J. (2002). *The Gospel of Mary Magdalene* (First Paperback Edition). Inner Traditions. (page 25)

[20] Contributors to Wikimedia projects. (2020, December 28). *Anthropos*. Wikipedia. https://en.wikipedia.org/wiki/Anthropos

Miryam was the one disciple who reached the same enlightenment level as Yeshua. This angered Peter and Andrew, who did not understand the message and were appalled that their Rabbi would share secret teachings with a woman. Unfortunately, many male disciples were too entrenched in their patriarchal, head-brain thinking and could not hear the messages with their hearts. In this limited thinking, the disciples parted, and many of the messages were not preached in the manner that Yeshua intended and taught. Peter called the rock by the early Christian church misunderstood messages, and this became the basis for the Christianity we know today in the Western Hemisphere.

Miryam understood and had achieved her purpose of realizing her fully human and fully divine incarnation. In her book, The Gospel of the Beloved Companion, The Complete Gospels of Mary, a translation by Jehanne De Quillan, published in 2010, the author states that the Gospel was preserved by her spiritual community based in France's Languedoc region (this is a crucial point to remember). DeQuillan proposes it is the complete version, unedited, of Mary's Gospel initially written in Greek in the first century. The author is unable to validate the texts she has translated; the originals have not been discovered. I felt this truth when I began reading; my heartbeat loudly and sped up each time I read a verse from this proposed Gospel. I have an apparent, distinct physical manifestation when I read spiritual information that resonates with me; I hear an electrical current loudly in both my ears; it is as though the Angels are encouraging me with their energy. The Aramaic language spoken by Yeshua and Miryam was meant to resonate within our bodies for our interpretations and meanings.

The popularity of Catharism in Southern France led to the Inquisition by Pope Innocent III and France's King in the twelfth century. This attack led to the destruction of this sect of Christianity who worshipped the feminine Holy Spirit. Cathar priests lived similar to monks, greatly influenced by the Essenes; they had no possessions and imposed no taxes on their congregations. Women and men were equals, and they believed that we continually incarnate into this world until we have reached enlightenment by denouncing all possessions in the material World, again, a solid Eastern influence. The Albigensian Crusade (1209-1229 CE) completely devastated their towns and cities, including a massacre in their church dedicated to Mary Magdalene; the church was almost entirely filled with women and children running for sanctuary. Once the attacks began, they were all burned alive within it. The Cathars rejected every aspect of the Roman Church and outwardly condemned the clergy for their greed and acquisitions of land and wealth; this labelled them heretics. Their popularity was viewed as a threat that needed to be extinguished. They held a deep belief that God had both a feminine and masculine principle; God's female aspect was Sophia (wisdom). The Beloved Companion's Gospel will be very familiar for readers who understand and can read between the lines of the Gospel of John in the New Testament of the canonical gospels; they both follow the exact chronology with similar words. The central contradiction lies in the name of "God." John's Gospel refers to the Heavenly Father, while the Gospel of the Beloved Companion uses the feminine Spirit, God the Mother. The Gospel of Mary in the Nag Hammadi Scriptures refers to this force as the Good. I will refer to this unnameable, infinite source of Love as Spirit, or Divine and sometimes Infinite Love/Source, replace with whatever resonates within you.

As I read the Gospel of the Beloved Companion and the various translations of The Gospel of Mary Magdalene and many of the Gospels in the Nag Hammadi of actual disciples who walked, prayed, and taught with the historical Yeshua, I felt the truth deep within my bones that the world would be a very different place had Miryam the Migdalah been honoured and had her rightful place as an enlightened master, teacher, wife and closest companion of her beloved Yeshua. Yeshua and Miryam's partnership and sacred sexual, deeply human relationship were examples for each of us. Our partners are our mirror selves; a profound message meant to assist each other in fully embracing our divine humanity and our divine soul essence. The denigration and silencing of Miryam and the divine Feminine was a blatant blasphemy to Spirit's other face and all of creation. Every living cell on Mother Earth has a feminine and masculine aspect: the sea creatures, four-legged, two-legged, and sky animals. The church has enforced a strictly male creator and deity, God the Father and his only Son. Mothers and daughters became pawns, property to be owned and dominated, bought and sold. This patriarchal, misogynist view has not only brought pain to females, but males and our Earth have also suffered tremendously.

> "The skies are broken
> Mother Earth cries out in pain
> The web of life mends."[21] (Mirabai Starr)

The sermon we are looking at by Miryam in the Gospel of the Beloved Companion and The Gospel of Mary is after the resurrection when the other disciples are caught up in ego, forgotten their divine selves, fearing for their lives, terrified of what might happen to them. In her full power as their leader, Miryam stands up and shares with them a secret teaching Yeshua gave only to her, another demonstration of their special love relationship, instructions that he had never shared with the others. This is where previously mentioned; Peter and Andrew get angry and do not believe that their Rabbi would share such information with a woman and not them. Yeshua was a radical freedom fighter, a revolutionary, a mystic. Mystics throughout history are known as reformers, and their messages are loud, outward announcements of how the divine invites us into her presence. Yeshua fully intended to shatter the status quo and rebel against Roman rule's hierarchy, informing the disciples that this hierarchy was not the truth. He deliberately shared secret, mystical teachings with a woman who understood and knew the all. In the first century, women were considered almost as lowly as slaves, not worthy. In leaving these secret teachings with Miryam, Yeshua instructs the disciples that the Roman hierarchy's egoic structure is false; we are all equal in the kingdom and Spirit. He also informs the disciples and all of us of the intimate relationship between him and Miryam. She is privy to secret teachings and can see him from within her pure heart. Here appears to be the first separation of the disciples and the Feminine removed from Christianity. It is evident in this passage that Miryam understood the inner teachings.

Peter and Andrew could not comprehend the learning because they were unwilling to release their stubborn attachment to their patriarchal

---

[21] Starr, M. (2019). *Wild Mercy: Living the Fierce and Tender Wisdom of the Women Mystics*. Sounds True.

upbringing. When the disciples parted to each go out into the world and share the good or Spirit, these teachings were lost to most Western world Christianity. Many theologians and scholars believe that John's Gospel was initially Mary Magdalene's writings and redacted to suppress her voice. As mentioned, the Gospels of Mary found in 1896 refer to the good, while the Beloved Companion's Gospel refers to Spirit. Again, never any mention of a Father God. Spirit is feminine, God the Mother, Heavenly Mother, wisdom. A male God figure was only reinforced in the New Testament during the council of Nicaea when the Nicene Creed was written, indicating One God the Father and One Begotten Son. "19 Then answered Jesus and said unto them, Verily, verily, I say unto you, The Son can★ do Nothing of himself, but what he seeth the Father do: for what things soever★ he doeth, these also doeth the Son likewise."[22] The GBC says "For whatever things the Spirit does, the Son does likewise."[23]

It is likely those who hid the papyrus that the gospels of Mary were written on; feared that if this information were to get into the wrong hands, they could prove deadly. Persecution of different sects of Christianity was utterly devastated for their gnosis beliefs or the Divine's direct experience. In addition to persecution, it is also likely that whoever removed the pages understood the message's enormity. Was humanity prepared for the incredible path that would lead to Heaven on Earth? Anyone who embarked on this path would discover no other authority than the Divine matters. All further control by the church, government or attachments to this physical existence would be meaningless once we find out the truth of our Divine connection. Most likely, monks from nearby monasteries tore out these pages and hid the rest, fearing the impact these teachings would have on ordinary folk, peasants who were not prepared to receive the Divine. This discovery

---

[22] Haynes, C. L., Jr, Haynes, C. L., Jr, Baker, L. L., & Danzey, E. (n.d.). *The Bible - Read and Study Free Online*. Bible Study Tools. Retrieved January 5, 2021, from https://www.biblestudytools.com/John 5:19

[23] Quillan, D. J. (2010). *The Gospel of the Beloved Companion: The Complete Gospel of Mary Magdalene*. CreateSpace Independent Publishing Platform.
Quillan, D. J. (2010). The Gospel of the Beloved Companion: The Complete Gospel of Mary Magdalene. CreateSpace Independent Publishing Platform GBC 13:19 (page 29)

would have created an upheaval to the "civilized" controlling approach the powers aimed to achieve.

Yeshua's teachings found in some of these apocryphal gospels are in direct defiance to the times' hierarchal system; they teach us that no authority has power over us outside ourselves and that we are all equal according to Spirit. The editors did not want the message of equality emphasized; it went against their hierarchy. It is evident in the canonical gospels that the apostle Paul may have had his words severely edited; he speaks at length in his letters about the prominent female ministers and commends them often. As it states in his letter to the Ephesians: "Wives, submit yourselves unto your own husbands, as unto the Lord. 23 For the husband is the head of the wife."[24] (Ephesians 5:22-24). Several quotes in the New Testament show Paul relaying these sentiments of the female as a lesser species and expected to be submissive; they claim women have no role in the Church's authority. Paul, originally Saul, who persecuted the followers of Yeshua and had an encounter with the risen Jesus to become an enlightened disciple, appears to have his words tampered with; they are contradictory in several locations.

As we move through these profound teachings, it is clear why these books would never make the New Testament cut. Firstly, it indicates a special relationship between Yeshua and Miryam, and secondly, it reveals that Miryam was a cherished disciple and an authority on the teachings of Yeshua, his equal. It also strongly suggests that a pope, bishops and priests are not necessary to achieve enlightenment; this would significantly diminish their power and wealth. Simon Peter said to Miryam in The Gospel of Mary Magdalene, "Sister, we know that the Teacher loved you more than any other woman. Tell us the words of the saviour that you remember, which you know, but we do not because we have not heard them."[25]

Similarly, the same sentiment in the Gospel of Phillip "loved Mary more than the disciples, and he often kissed her on the mouth …

---

[24] Haynes, C. L., Jr, Haynes, C. L., Jr, Baker, L. L., & Danzey, E. (n.d.). *The Bible - Read and Study Free Online*. Bible Study Tools. Retrieved January 5, 2021, from https://www.biblestudytools.com/Ephesians 5:22-24

[25] Meyer, M. W., & Boer, E. D. A. (2006). *The Gospels of Mary: The Secret Tradition of Mary Magdalene, the Companion of Jesus*. HarperOne. (page 20)

"[26] (Phillip 63.34–36.) In the Gnostic tradition, a kiss on the mouth represented the breath of Spirit and knowledge. In exchanging this kiss, Yeshua indicates that Miryam is his equal and will continue to spread the good news as an authority after his death. Yeshua initiated her as the Nazarenes leader (what these first disciples were, Christianity did not exist yet). We know Yeshua was a rebel and did not care about dogma, but laws within Judaism prohibit any touching between men and women who are not married, unless parents or siblings. In the mystery schools where Yeshua and Miryam likely studied, the hieros gamos, sacred relational love, was a soul mate union and a path leading to the Divine. Many of these ancient teachings taught that the soul was split into two and placed into different bodies, one female and one male; this is also indicated in the book of Genesis in the Old Testament canonical gospels. This separation is the longing throughout lifetimes to find the twin flame, beloved soul mate. It is also a mystical inference of the reuniting of our true nature's masculine and feminine aspects within our hearts. In the Gospel of Phillip translation by Jean-Yves Leloup, the Gospel describes the bridal chamber as a reunion of Adam and Eve after the fall, separating the masculine and Feminine.[27] The fully human aspects of Yeshua and Miryam would indeed include a healthy, deeply connected sexuality. The Gospel of Phillip describes a sacred sexual union (as in marriage or exclusive partnership) as "the holy of holies." "The mystery which unites two beings is great; without it, the world would not exist."[28] While there is no valid information in writing at this time, we can hear with our hearts and feel the truth for ourselves. In addition to considering their exceptional love for one another on a physical and spiritual level, it is essential to recognize Miryam's dedication and status as a fully realized human and divine. An Ihidaya, unified one when the heart becomes focused entirely on

[26] Meyer, M. W., Pagels, E. H., Robinson, J. M., Funk, W., & Poirier, P. (2009). *The Nag Hammadi Scriptures: The Revised and Updated Translation of Sacred Gnostic Texts Complete in One Volume* (1st ed.). HarperOne. (The Gospel of Phillip 63.34–36)

[27] Leloup, J., Rowe, J., & Needleman, J. (2004). *The Gospel of Philip: Jesus, Mary Magdalene, and the Gnosis of Sacred Union* (Illustrated ed.). Inner Traditions.

[28] Leloup, J., Rowe, J., & Needleman, J. (2002). *The Gospel of Mary Magdalene* (First Paperback Edition). Inner Traditions. (Mary 10:2:6) page 31

living and acting only through the Divine spark within. The bridal chamber is a state of consciousness, a sacred state inside the heart. Only when our higher consciousness is ready may we be given grace in kairos, divine perfect timing. This state of being is achieved in receiving the most extraordinary possible grace, and a partner on the same path can enhance this state.

These found gospels show us the earliest Christian movements, where female disciples held equal status amongst the males. We cannot dispute the Gospels of Phillip because we know even from the New Testament canonical gospels that Phillip was one of the earliest disciples of Yeshua's ministry. He had been a disciple of John the Baptist. Matthew 10:3 and Luke 6:14 name him as the fifth disciple to Yeshua. Therefore, we know he walked with Yeshua throughout his ministry and had firsthand knowledge of his teachings. Of the four canonical gospels Matthew/Levi was the only disciple who had firsthand knowledge of Christ.

Simon Peter, before becoming angry, also turns to Miryam as an authority of the teachings of their Rabbi, as indicated previously. He acknowledges that she understands and knows the teachings and asks her to share her knowledge with the other disciples who either do not know them or have not grasped their meaning. We find this also in the Dialogue of the Saviour in the Nag Hammadi Scriptures; "Mary utters words of wisdom. Mary said, "So the wickedness of each day is sufficient. Workers deserve their food. Disciples resemble their teachers. She spoke this utterance as a woman who understood completely." [29] Miryam is an authority and beloved disciple who walked the talk and achieved the Feminine Christ consciousness while embodied.

In the Gospel of John at the Last Supper, Jesus speaks to his disciples, "He that hath my commandments, and keepeth them, he it is that loveth me: and he that loveth me shall be loved of my Father, and I will love him, and will manifest myself to him. Judas saith unto him, not Iscariot, Lord, how is it that thou wilt manifest thyself unto us, and not unto the world? Jesus answered and said unto him, If a man love me, he will

---

[29] Meyer, M. W., Pagels, E. H., Robinson, J. M., Funk, W., & Poirier, P. (2009). *The Nag Hammadi Scriptures: The Revised and Updated Translation of Sacred Gnostic Texts Complete in One Volume* (1ˢᵗ ed.). HarperOne. (139,8-13).

keep my words: and my Father will love him, and we will come unto him, and make our abode with him. He that loveth me not keepeth not my sayings: and the word which ye hear is not mine, but the Father's which sent me."[30] (John 14:21-24)

The Gospel of the Beloved Companion shares a radically different speech. Yeshua specifically appoints Miryam as the leader of the Nazarenes and the one disciple who has shown that she is Ihidaya keeping the commandments, understanding the true meaning of love and living in Spirit. "The Disciples said to Yeshua, "When will you depart from us? Who is to be our leader?" And Yeshua said to them, "I will not leave you orphans. When a father goes away, it is the mother who tends the children."[31] (GBC 35:16.)

The Gospel of John and The Gospel of the Beloved Companion state that he will ``manifest" or ``reveal`` himself to the loved one who keeps his commandments. That this person loves him, and he loves them. In The Gospel of the Beloved Companion, it is clear that Miryam, as the mother, is to be the leader of the disciples; he specifically appoints her in the presence of all of the followers. Perhaps the canonical gospels' editors did not have faith that the readers would relate or put these together when they kept in that Mary Magdalene was the first Jesus manifested himself on the third day. Alternatively, perhaps because she was a woman, they felt it did not matter, clearly her significance at this incredible event could not be omitted entirely. It is quite simple to compare these texts and see that there are "partial" truths in the New Testament; it is also very apparent to see where the editors completely suppressed Miryam's involvement and importance. In the Gospel of John, Judas asks him how he will manifest to them and not to the entire world; we now know it would be through a pure heart capable of witnessing his risen self with their inner vision. Experiencing divine wisdom within our hearts was not a teaching the Romans would want

---

[30] Haynes, C. L., Jr, Haynes, C. L., Jr, Baker, L. L., & Danzey, E. (n.d.). *The Bible - Read and Study Free Online.* Bible Study Tools. Retrieved January 5, 2021, from https://www.biblestudytools.com/John 14:21-24

[31] Quillan, D. J. (2010). *The Gospel of the Beloved Companion: The Complete Gospel of Mary Magdalene.* CreateSpace Independent Publishing Platform. 35:16 (page 65)

to be revealed. This would have stripped them of any authority over the peoples' Spiritual lives.

Yeshua informs his disciples that he appoints Miryam as his ministry's authority when he is gone. He names her L Magdallah or the Magdalene, which translates in English to tower, stronghold or keeper of the flocks. Yeshua called her this to elevate her status among the disciples. It is evident that Peter the Rock was not appointed by Yeshua because he had not reached the enlightenment and understanding of the teachings in the way Miryam had. Interestingly, in Hebrew mysticism, the letter H, which is added to MagdallaH, the ladder is called the Sephiroth, mystical tree (which we will go into more detail later.) Margaret Starbird clarifies, "Magdalene's Aramaic title implies greatness, exaltation, elevation and pre-eminence."[32]

Yeshua guides Miryam through an inner vision (meditation) or gnosis (internal knowledge) to become fully human and fully divine in this embodiment. The Church fathers later edited this to become seven demons Jesus cast out of her as wickedness. Hence, this is how Pope Gregory, in the year 591CE in his homily 33, assumed that Mary Magdalene must have been a prostitute. ★[33] As we will see from the Gospel of the Beloved Companion, The Gospel of Mary Magdalene and many of the found apocryphal gospels, Miryam was far from wicked; she was in all rights Yeshua's equal. Many of the apocryphal gospels found at Nag Hammadi refer to Yeshua speaking of himself as a mentor or teacher. Once the student reaches the same level of enlightenment, they are identical. Much confusion happened with scholars when the Gospel of Thomas referred to him as Yeshua's twin. It was not referring to a blood sibling; it referred to a state of consciousness within the disciple. The student had become the teacher and, therefore, his brother or sister in Spirit. In the Gospel of Thomas, Yeshua explains that we all received our being from the same source and, therefore, all can have all things revealed to us. Jesus said, "He who will drink from my mouth

---

[32] Starbird, M. (2009). *Sacred Union in Christianity*. Margaretstarbird.Net. http://margaretstarbird.net

[33] The Roman Catholic Church, Pope Paul VI removed the depiction of Mary Magdalene as a prostitute in 1969. Unfortunately, many people are still unaware of this and continue to consider her a penitent sinner.

will become like me. I myself shall become he, and the things that are hidden will be revealed to him."[34] Yeshua's lessons continually taught about creation's oneness, never elevating himself above any being or creature. Each of us is valuable and equal; we teach and learn from one another, not in arrogance or superiority; in humble reverence to our Creator to assist in the evolution of humanity and embrace love.

Yeshua prophesied at the last supper that the person he revealed himself to, the Spirit, would also complete in all ways. This guided inner vision reveals to Miryam how to live a fully embodied human life while also listening for guidance and support from our divine self. The lesson is not to allow the ego and the head-brain to lead us or have power over us and how we can move into the nous (the spiritual heart) and the unity consciousness of Spirit. In the Gospel of Thomas, Jesus says: "Whoever finds the world and becomes rich, let him renounce the world."[35] The teaching is not about denying our human side as many churches proclaim a sin; it is about learning to recognize when the ego is in charge, go to the silence, and see where we can replace the darkness with light. Mother Earth and descending into the physical world are necessary to train our spiritual muscles and evolve. This is a shamanic experience, an inner body experience of discovering what emotions or ego energies need to be transformed to ascend and realize we are children of the living Spirit, Mother. Speaking of a shamanic experience, the Hebrew word for oil is shemen ha mishcha (ha'mishcha), an anointing oil used to anoint priests and kings. The bride also used this anointing oil to anoint the bridegroom king. The Hebrew word is a similar word to a shaman, one who knows using the awareness of the Earth, Spirit, Plants, everything on Earth has consciousness. Altering human consciousness from ordinary earthly reality to a connected, activated level aware of Spirit is a deeply personal, internal journey. Often, special oils assist with accessing information from a higher level of awareness, a way of cocreation; Miryam was the anointer, the bride Queen.

---

[34] Meyer, M. W., Pagels, E. H., Robinson, J. M., Funk, W., & Poirier, P. (2009). *The Nag Hammadi Scriptures: The Revised and Updated Translation of Sacred Gnostic Texts Complete in One Volume* (1st ed.). HarperOne. (Gospel of Thomas saying 108).
[35] Ibid 34. (The Gospel of Thomas saying 110).

As Miryam continues to ascend each level, she feels her soul embraced by this brilliant creatrix, Mother of All. She declares that we momentarily forget our authentic divine selves, and our purpose is to reclaim our divine lineage while embodied. When we arrive in this Earth realm, our soul descends into a physical body. We are raised and live-in communities of people who have forgotten who they are. We believe our bodies and this material 3D World are our whole reality. As we pray and meditate, we begin to awaken, and we remember we are both a body and a soul and our souls are connected to the Infinite Spirit. We cannot be separate; we just forgot for a moment, and I believe this is the whole point of this existence, to remember our connection. Everything in the Universe is part of the one. It is time for us to see through the illusion of separateness and shed our attachments to the ego and physical world. We are not instructed to discard our humanity or leave our physical beings unattended; it only directs us to detach from the hold that temporary things have over us. We create pain and suffering when we believe this is all we are. When we embody our true nature as fully human and fully divine, we can fulfill our purpose on the earth realm and spread love, light and kindness. Our physical bodies become the vessel we use to share the good news with all. Our souls are our masters, intuitively connecting and following the guidance from within, we will fulfill our soul's purpose during this lifetime; to be in service to each other and all of creation. Mary's gospel is a living testimony we can use every day to realize our true humanity.

My Soul Speaks

Bring light to the darkness. Open your heart to only love. Release fear and know that you are constantly being guided; you always have love and support. Your only job is to be kind, compassionate and loving. Allow life to flow through you and see the world only through the lens of love. There are many on Earth needlessly suffering. It is time.

Affirmation

The Divine Universe employs me to speak the truth and shine a light on the darkness; all my needs are met.

Exercise

If you have a diffuser and essential oils, I always put five drops of each Frankincense, myrrh and rose essential oil in my diffuser to invoke Yeshua and Miryam into my space. Alternatively, you can drop each onto a cotton ball and breathe in the scents.

Have your pen and journal beside you as you once again enter your heart space. Close your eyes and take three full breaths; in through the nose and out through the mouth, feeling any tension leave your body in the deep exhales.

Visualize from your heart space Yeshua and Miryam before you, embracing you in a beautiful golden-white light.

Ask them for their assistance in shining light on the areas in your life where there is darkness—the parts of you where you perhaps feel unworthy of divine love. Feel deeply into the darkness and feel the light of these Ascended Masters infuse the parts of yourself you deem unfit with love and forgiveness and the light of eternal life.

Thank them for their unconditional love, guidance, and support and gently open your eyes when you are ready.

Spend time journaling with the 10 minutes free writing exercise; no editing or stopping; just pouring out your thoughts and feelings.

Repeat this exercise as often as necessary to embrace all parts of yourself, light and shadow, knowing that our creator loves All of our beings.

CHAPTER 6

THE ONE WHO UNDERSTANDS

ONCE THE DISCIPLES HAVE ASKED MIRYAM TO TELL THEM WHAT the Rabbi has taught her what they did not remember or know, she begins with a teaching so profound and utterly unheard of in any known Christian texts. She speaks of an inner vision, a place within her where she witnesses her beloved Rabbi even after death. A testament that we live in a multidimensional universe, our energy, our divine spark, lives beyond this realm of physical matter.

"My master spoke thus to me. He said, ``There is a great tree within you that does not change, Summer or Winter, and its leaves do not fall. Whosoever listens to my words and ascends its crown will not taste death."[36]

In this passage, Yeshua is commending Miryam for her dedication to his teachings and diligently keeping to her spiritual practices to receive the atonement of the kingdom. Our current worldview fears death because we are so attached to the mental ego; the ego knows that when a person dies, it dies with it. So what lives is our Divine Self, the eternal us that is cyclical. One of Yeshua's greatest teachings to humanity was not only how to live but how to die to the ego-self while still living. To live in non-dual consciousness, knowing that life and death are not separate; they are part of the whole, self-realization of unifying our inner and outer worlds. According to Meggan Watterson, the word death, translated from Aramaic to English, is to exist elsewhere, to not

---

[36] Quillan, D. J. (2010). *The Gospel of the Beloved Companion: The Complete Gospel of Mary Magdalene.* CreateSpace Independent Publishing Platform. 42:2 (page 116)

be in the present moment. It is a separation of the soul and body, the soul and Infinite Source. To come into knowing our Spiritual being, we must recognize the Earthly being for what it is; temporary. We must also know that our souls cannot be here in this embodiment without the body. The body is the vessel that allows the soul to have this experience. In the Gospel of Thomas, Jesus repeats this "Jesus said, the heavens and the Earth will be rolled up in your presence. And the one who lives from the living one will not see death. Does not Jesus say, whoever finds himself is superior to the world."[37] To come into being before coming into being; is a reference to the knowledge of one's true nature, listening to the self within and not identifying with the ego and the limiting beliefs of duality. Miryam knew that she existed before her current physical incarnation and will continue to exist beyond it as part of the One; her inner eye of the heart is set upon discovering the queendom of heaven within and witnessing it in all of creation.

Using the symbol of a tree is once again a reference to the mystery school teachings and the tree of life that dates back to the ancient Egyptian teachings. The tree of life is a universal symbol that has been used in religion and spirituality for many centuries. It represents interconnectedness with the entire Universe, unity consciousness. The roots grow deep into Mother Earth while the branches reach high up into the heavens. It was often depicted in the ancient womb mysteries as a symbol of fertility and family. To this day, we still use a tree to symbolize a family tree. It is also a symbol of Miryam's individuality, as each tree is unique. In this case, it describes her personal spiritual growth. The tree also symbolizes eternal life, a prominent theme in early Christian teachings. A tree loses its leaves in the Fall, and they come back in the Spring. When a tree ages, it sprouts seedlings, and new trees grow. Life is cyclical, and material things die only for new life to be reborn.

Jesus in Revelations says, "He that hath an ear, let him hear what the Spirit saith unto the churches; To him that overcometh will I give

---

[37] Meyer, M. W., Pagels, E. H., Robinson, J. M., Funk, W., & Poirier, P. (2009). *The Nag Hammadi Scriptures: The Revised and Updated Translation of Sacred Gnostic Texts Complete in One Volume* (1ˢᵗ ed.). HarperOne. (The Gospel of Thomas p. 154, saying 111).

to eat of the tree of life, which is in the midst of the paradise of God."[38] (Revelation 2:7) He commands us to listen to the silence within to hear what the Spirit is saying. The paradise of Source is right here, on Earth, and as we overcome our attachments to our ego, we are gifted with the fruits of our Creatrix. When we eat the fruit and live our lives according to the higher virtues, we live in peace and reflect the light of the Divine from our beings, and we become the image of Infinite Love we were created to be. The Kabbalistic tree of life is a guide to understanding the flow of energy from the Infinite to physical, ways creative energy flows, and awareness with the ten Sefirah (flow of energy.) The tree of life symbol asks us to consider the soul's higher purpose beyond our limited physical reality. The tree asks humans to be aware of the interconnectedness of all life on our survival, ourselves, and the entire planet we live on. The Token Rock Inspiration Centre describes it as "a mystical symbol within the Kabbalah of esoteric Judaism. 'The Tree of life is considered to be a map of the universe and the psyche, the order of the creation of the cosmos, and a path to spiritual illumination."[39]

Interestingly, the early kabbalah masters who designated the position and concept of each Sefirah lived in Southern France in the twelfth century, the same time as the Cathars thrived in the area and where the Gospel of the Beloved Companion was in circulation. It is also where Miryam was an essential teacher of the Way in the first century when she was forced into exile from Roman persecution, according to legend. There is a myth that she arrived on a ship with no sails and no oars, along with Mother Mary, Mary of Bethany and an Egyptian slave-girl named Sarah. Many legends suggest Sarah is the beloved child of Miryam and Yeshua, a beautiful soul with healing powers, and this is understandable as priestesses surround her. Sarah-La-Kali (Sarah the black) is still honoured, and festivals are held to pay her reverence; on May 24, she is considered the Queen of the Outsiders by the Romani

---

[38] Haynes, C. L., Jr, Haynes, C. L., Jr, Baker, L. L., & Danzey, E. (n.d.). *The Bible - Read and Study Free Online*. Bible Study Tools. Retrieved January 5, 2021, from https://www.biblestudytools.com/Revelation 2:7

[39] Tree of Life. (n.d.). *Tree of Life - A Thorough Explanation*. Token Rock. Retrieved February 1, 2021, from https://www.tokenrock.com/explain-tree-of-life-160.html

(gypsy) people. The material world is a small fraction of one experience the infinite soul has on Earth. Birth, death, rebirth is a continuous cycle, with no beginning and no end. We are constantly reminded to look to nature for the meaning of life; we can gain a great perspective as to our place in this existence. We are natural, cyclical, immortal, and each of us is on our unique path of reuniting with our spiritual nature. In the New Testament, Jesus calls the higher state of ascended consciousness "the tree of life." "… To him that overcometh will I give to eat of the tree of life, which is in the midst of the paradise of God"[40]. In overcoming our fleshly desires and transforming them to heavenly desires, we may eat from the tree of life and realize our everlasting nature.

The Gospel of Mary Magdalene and The Gospel of the Beloved Companion leads us into an inner vision Miryam sees with the heart's eye. She can experience the risen Yeshua with her inner vision because of the love that transcends death.

Many scholars have presented a theory that Yeshua spent his first years travelling and learning from many great masters throughout the East and the Essenes of Judea. However, mainstream Christianity says very little about these first thirty years of his life other than him being a carpenter. If we, as Yeshua instructed, have the ears to hear, we should listen, which indicates to me that we must listen to the unspoken words and the language in which he speaks; with our inner ear, our nous/eye of the heart. If Yeshua did indeed learn in the mystery schools and other eastern spirituality, he would be very familiar with energy healing and the importance of the chakras or energy centres in our physical and spiritual health. The roots of this tree are our root chakra, the energy centre at the base of our spine that keeps us grounded to the Earthly realm, our body. As we move through the other five chakras referred to here as the "five regions of humanity,"[41] the sacral, solar plexus, heart, throat and third eye, we continue to move away from our physical matter closer to the Spirit realms to finally reach the crown chakra and

---

[40] Haynes, C. L., Jr, Haynes, C. L., Jr, Baker, L. L., & Danzey, E. (n.d.). *The Bible - Read and Study Free Online*. Bible Study Tools. Retrieved January 5, 2021, from https://www.biblestudytools.com/Revelation 2:7

[41] Quillan, D. J. (2010). *The Gospel of the Beloved Companion: The Complete Gospel of Mary Magdalene*. CreateSpace Independent Publishing Platform. 42:3 (page 116)

our connection to the ethereal kingdom of Heaven, our higher self. The tree is our body, and each bough symbolizes our energetic chakra system, with the root, sacral and solar plexus chakras looking after our physical identity and our relationship with the physical world. These chakras keep us grounded and, when balanced, a healthy connection with the physical realm. The upper chakras, throat, third eye and crown unite us with Infinite Source. The heart in the middle is the bridge between the material and the spiritual; herein resides the nous. Only when balanced, can we live as fully human and fully divine beings.

Yeshua mentions the crown twice through the verses in these teachings as the kingdom of the spirit, our connection to the Divine. As we ascend upwards from the heart chakra (our soul centre or nous, where divine consciousness resides), we begin to become aligned with our Divine nature. This is not about transcending or having an out-of-body experience; this is about connecting fully within our body and connecting with our soul. Our throat is where we express our soul's gifts; our third eye, our inner knowing or higher consciousness and finally, our crown, where we experience the flow of life in connection to All that is and our knowledge of the oneness of all of creation. Our crown chakra is where we are cocreators with Spirit and live freely in limitless possibilities and unconditional love. To live a balanced life, we have an ego that keeps us grounded in our human existence. We also have a soul that is connected to Infinite Light. Living too much in either creates an imbalance. Our purpose is to realize and embrace all aspects of our being without making attachments.

As we progress through each bough, each guardian represents an ego power; this is challenged by the opposite energies of the soul desire. As we grow spiritually and remember who we are, the lower ego attachments are released and replaced with higher divine emotions. The guardian at each gate is our ego trying to keep us small and continue to live in the illusion of separateness. We must fully transform our lower ego desires from personal wants and needs to divine wishes for the greatest good of all to be considered worthy of continuing along our spiritual path. This is the meaning of resurrection; each day, each moment is another opportunity for us to try again. The ego's guardians or powers will continually challenge us, and by staying conscious and aware, we have the chance to go within and choose again. We need the ego to encounter all that it means to be fully human; being human is an incredible opportunity for us to grow and evolve. We must also remember we are a soul, and we have the freedom (free will) to make conscious decisions, knowing when the ego is trying to bind us.

The guardian at each bough is our fears and doubts that we are not worthy of direct connection with the Divine or have the ability to have authority over our own lives. We no longer trust ourselves or our inner guidance because the outside powers for generations have controlled us. This path is an incredible opportunity to regularly check in with our souls for the most accurate advice. These fears have been so ingrained in us over the centuries that not only do we have to heal our shadows, in doing so, we recover our ancestor's traumas and release the "karma" of these false beliefs for future generations. We have been led to believe for more than two millennia that being human is wrong, sinful and that the body is inherently bad; the soul cannot have this experience without the flesh. If we had no ego, no body, the soul would not be able to have this magnificent experience in the matter. In realizing our soul's power, we are reminded of our divine nature. Each bough prepares us for an ever-deepening awareness and closer to direct communication with Spirit. The ego represents the false powers of this world, money, status, job; anything that has authority over us or has the ability to create needless pain and suffering. This also includes memories that we cannot release because we "identify" with them, be they past hurts, betrayals or emotional trauma that we hold onto to stay victimized. If we are no longer a victim to these memories, who are we? When we forgive ourselves or others, our unconscious selves or egos are misled to believe we are giving our power away, and we give up the perception of control. In truth, forgiveness is the most powerful, freeing force in the Universe. Often, when I am unable or unwilling to forgive in a moment, perhaps the pain is too great, and I have not worked through it, I will ask the Divine to send love on my behalf. I will pray, "Please understand I am not there yet; I know this person deserves love and forgiveness; if you do this for me until I have worked out my shit, that would be greatly appreciated!"

I was well into my forties when I finally released the belief that I was not smart enough from something my father said within my earshot when I was sixteen years old. I recalled him telling a family friend how shocked he was that I received such high school grades. He then explained that my elder brother Danny was a genius and I an airhead. I carried that wound with me for almost thirty years and allowed it to hold me back in many areas, especially my career, for fear that others may discover I was not as bright as I appeared to be. When I finally faced this shadow part of this misconception or false belief, I realized that in my father's perception of me as an "airhead," it was actually that I longed for peace, compassion and kindness in the chaotic world of an alcoholic upbringing. I often retreated into this "heavenly" place within myself when the outside world became too much for me. This may have appeared flaky, but it was a coping mechanism to retreat from the physical world I did not feel safe in or that I could not escape. When I was truly dedicated to changing my life and moved out of the density that this power had over my life and held it into the light, forgiveness of both myself and my father transformed the dense matter into love.

The first three boughs on the path are about detachment from the powers we believe are our authority; we cannot serve two masters. Then, as we step onto the way of enlightened life, we get to choose; will we give our power away and serve the temporary, earthly, material world? Or our eternal self, our soul with a wholehearted faith in the unseen power of Infinite Source?

GBC 42:5 "Those who seek to climb must free themselves of the world."[42]

When we are firmly grounded in the material world, we cannot see the Oneness in the Universe. We function entirely led by our ego, where we compete, judge, and only see others as different from us. If we access Miryam as our teacher and guide and move into our heart and our I AM presence; the light can reach us and guide our way. As we move farther away from identification with our ego and the material world, we are freed to experience our eternal selves of Spirit. Many Eastern religions believe we reincarnate into new physical bodies several times to evolve our soul until we have finally released the belief that

---

[42] Ibid 41. 42:5 (page 117)

the material world is who we are. Once we have finally released our attachment, we are free to finally rest our souls from this earthly realm and return to the One consciousness Spirit for all of eternity.

Interestingly, the Torah describes Jacobs's ladder as an ascension to the Heavenly realms or a stairway to Heaven. In his dream, Jacob sees a reunion with Heaven and Earth. There have been many interpretations of this; in Christianity, it is said Jesus brought the vision into reality. The heart is a path for all of us to unite Heaven and Earth within by trying in each moment to live a virtuous life. This is not a climb upwards toward a realm beyond physical death; it is a climb inwards to discover our authentic selves as divine beings having a human experience, thus uniting our whole selves.

With its limitations, gratitude for a fully human experience opens us to an opportunity to have a beautiful life while in the Earthly realm. When we practice non-attachment to every occasion, we surrender the outcome and remove an event's judgment as good or bad; life flows through us. We become cocreators with Spirit and raise our vibrational frequency to attract life and all that we need to experience and embody for our souls to evolve. As we step onto the path together, I honour everyone who dares to do the work necessary to live our most meaningful life and fulfill our soul's potential. I encourage you to take as much time on each bough as required and to return to them as often as you feel is needed. I find that there are days when I have to return to specific exercises more often than others because the shadow side is far more ingrained in my subconscious. However, as I practice at least once each day; or remind myself throughout the day (yes, several times), I grow closer to my authentic self and speak my truth more often.

Miryam's path was the way of the heart; she was a devoted disciple of Yeshua and, in his own words, his equal. She lived a life in service to Spirit, the good or whatever feels most appropriate to you when speaking of the Divine. She was a threat to the early church because she did not conform to their dogmas or rituals; she was firmly rooted in her earthly incarnation while also being devoted to embodying her fully divine self. I invite you to embark on this journey with Miryam; through daily prayer and meditation and fulfill your soul's purpose of living a fully human and fully divine life.

My Soul Speaks

In a fitful sleep, worrying about the future, primarily the material future in a time of so much uncertainty in the economy, I heard a soft, gentle voice reminding me that life only exists in the present moment, the eternal Now. This voice guided me to go within and be assured that all was well, that at this moment, everything was as it should be. Death in Aramaic, Yeshua and Miryam's language translates as existing elsewhere. When we obsess about the future or live in the past, we are not fully alive. We are only alive in the present moment, the Now.

Affirmation

I embrace my fully human experience and know that I have the freedom to make choices every day for the greatest good of all. When negative feelings or emotions enter, I will remember to go within and remember I am also a soul.

Exercise

Gratitude is one of life's most precious gifts; the more we express gratitude; we raise our vibrational frequency to attract more of which to be grateful for into our lives. There is always a rainbow; we may not always see its colours if we are in the middle of something we judge as suffering, but the light will appear and dissolve the darkness in divine timing.

Keep a journal that is entirely used for gratitude. Decorate it with inspirational words or artwork. Several journals on the market are now specifically reserved and labelled as a Gratitude Journal if this inspires you.

Before retiring for the night, open your journal, date it at the top and write down ten things that happened throughout the day that you are grateful for. You can number these or categorize them, Work, Family, Friends.

In the morning, read the list from the previous evening. A good exercise is to take a meditative walk thinking of your gratitude list as your "mantras." Repeat them as you walk (I guarantee a smile will automatically form!)

If you struggled to develop ten things, explore areas in your life where you can create things to be grateful for. If you could not find something at work, what can you do today to create something? Perhaps a colleague never gets invited for lunch with others; could you ask them and get to know them better? Often, when we do something for others, we can be grateful for the opportunity and extend the chance for that person to have something to be thankful for.

CHAPTER 7

MIRYAM THE MYRROPHORE

MYRROPHORE WAS A MISTRESS OF THE OILS, A PRE-BIBLICAL Egyptian temple tradition of women bearing myrrh. Mary Magdalene is depicted in the canonical gospels carrying her alabaster jar of spikenard and anointing Jesus' feet before the crucifixion. If this were the anointing oil Mary brought, Spikenard would have been used to increase Jesus' spiritual connection and open his heart to connect with the nature of the Divine. Her skills as a healer priestess, a soul healer, were vital to his mission of radically transforming hearts, guiding us back to the power of love within ourselves and a profoundly deep connection with our Creator. This anointing is also what led Pope Gregory to declare that she must have been a prostitute. Instead of recognizing our ancestors' natural healing abilities using anointing oils, he suggested a perfume potion she used to put on her body to attract clients. He could not have been further from the truth, in his ignorance, he set in motion a lie that would last centuries. Myrrophores were priestesses skilled at assisting people with the death transition from an earthly body to our infinite light body and were master healers of the body and soul. Miryam and her priestesses, including Mother Mary, had a primary purpose in the life of Yeshua, assisting him in staying connected with his authentic soul essence and healing from within. The brief mentions in the canonical gospels are a hidden message for those who had the eyes to see her true power in her own rights as an initiated priestess and healer. The priestesses were trained from a young age in Isis's temple with intense initiations in energy healing, alchemy and transition through death, physical and spiritual rebirth.

Interestingly, the apocryphal gospels share a radically different Yeshua from the canonical gospels. This profoundly spiritual man did not want to found a religion or be called the Son of God. His and Miryam's sole purpose was to serve humanity in raising consciousness through soul healing, helping us awaken to the divine within us. The wisdom of the heart and soul using sacred anointing oils helps connect to Divine energy. Ancient Egyptians believed that inhaling certain oils increased our energetic frequency, which enabled us to commune with the Divine. All Hebrew kings and priests were anointed with the elixir of the Gods, and this was done for cleansing and purification, awakening them to be in service to God and appointing them as called ones or chosen ones. The oils were said to elevate them to higher consciousness in connection with God. Panacea was a Greek goddess, daughter of Asclepius and Epione; she is mentioned at the beginning of the Hippocratic Oath. Known as a goddess of healing, she is depicted carrying a magic potion that could cure all illnesses. Miryam's skills as a healer, with her anointing oils, were essential to the alchemical transmutation Yeshua went through to reach the spiritual state of unity consciousness, in harmony with the Divine.

Anointing someone is a sacred act of devotion, healing the soul through divine intelligence. Oils are mentioned several times about Jesus in the canonical gospels, but the greatest of all is Miryam and her priestess sisters at the crucifixion and following the body to the tomb with her alabaster jar. Miryam was anointing Yeshua in the canonical gospels to soothe his soul and spirit, and the event mentioned was not the only occasion in which Miryam performed this act. Their work on this Earth was intense and would have taken a tremendous toll on his body and soul. Miryam helped release negative energies and emotional blocks in anointing him, continually assisting him reconnecting with his divine self. Anointing his feet is even more significant in her knowledge of healing with sacred oils. Our feet absorb the oils into our bodies the fastest, and in studying reflexology, our feet are connected with every internal organ. We also pick up energy, negative and positive, through our feet, and we know Yeshua walked with and healed the most broken souls; this energy would accumulate in the feet. Miryam revitalizes his power to flow freely, enabling him to continue his healing work proficiently. Healing others with the intensity that Yeshua did would often deplete the healer of energy, sometimes physical, other times emotional or etheric. The physical world's density and the chaos and violence of the times would be taxing for a lightworker of his magnitude. We see this with empaths even today, other people's emotional density often affects deep emotions in their hearts, and they feel others' energy in their bodies and souls. This is yet another glimpse into the importance of Miryam's work during this significant time of lifting humanity out of the darkness. She was not only a favoured disciple; Yeshua could not have done his work on the physical realm without her by his side. Miryam healed his body and soul, and her role was vital in him completing his mission here. She was a powerful healer who quite possibly used her anointing oils to prepare him as all Hebrew kings and priests, which strengthened his physical power and spiritual power in preparation for the crucifixion act.

I have recently been working for the past few years with essential oils derived from healing plants. It has become a sideline passion for me, and I have created many healing concoctions. We have pre-made jars throughout our home for each family member, from sinus congestion, cough and cold, menstruation pain and more recently, a pain reliever for arthritis. I continue to study with teachers who have experimented with oils for many years and choose oils through quiet prayer and contemplating what is best for a particular ailment. Each day before I begin writing, I invoke Yeshua and Miryam at my altar with prayer and put Rose oil, Frankincense and myrrh in my diffuser. Rose is often associated with Mary Magdalene; it is said that when they discovered her tomb in the year 1279 in France and opened it, a wonderful smell of perfume filled the air with the scent of roses. Frankincense and myrrh were gifted to the baby Yeshua at his birth according to the gospels, and they both hold countless healing properties.

Miryam had been trained her entire life in the Mystery school traditions. In these traditions, initiates' powers are discovered and then harnessed for the greatest good of all. An initiate may have a natural inclination for herbal remedies and spend their days learning this gift to bring it out into the world. Miryam would have studied rigorously in energy work, divine energy. In the same way, Yeshua could heal, Miryam would have had the same abilities with her unique healing powers. During his ministry, the women in Yeshua's life were all in some way related to him, except, of course, in the canonical gospels Mary Magdalene. We can assume from this that there is a possible relationship between Yeshua and Miryam, or else, where did she come from, and how did she arrive to become the most prominent Mary next to him? The confusion of the many Marys is explained from those mystery schools. A high priestess of Isis's Mystery Schools would very likely earn Mary's title once she had completed her initiations. It was a name of honour and respect; Mary Anna (the mother of Yeshua), Mary Magdalene (the partner of Yeshua), Mary Salome (Helena; aunt of Yeshua.). These are only a few of the many female disciples vaguely mentioned in the canonical gospels. Mary Anna (Mother Mary) and Miryam would have collaborated and supported Yeshua throughout his life and ministry as spiritual leaders surrounded by devoted priestesses.

The Mary's are a holy order, and their teachings are rooted in the feminine, in love and union, union within us, the Divine and all of creation. The Mary title comes from the Egyptian Mer, water, sea, which is the crucial symbol for an Isis priestess. Miryam represents the divine feminine energy returning to earth after thousands of years of distortion as both a human woman and spiritual energy, restoring power to all of us. Our collective consciousness is awakening to the divine feminine Christ, and Mary Magdalene is an archetype for this energy; Yeshua represents the masculine Christ consciousness. Through these lost gospels, we can relate to both their humanity and the path they taught to reach this state of consciousness as cocreators, mastering both feminine and masculine energies of the universe and within each of us. Yeshua and Miryam were equal ministers, modelling humanity's path to enlightenment. Yeshua led Peter and the male disciples to teach the outer church, speaking publicly to the people. Miryam would lead the gnostic (inner knowing) secrets to those prepared to receive the more profound knowledge along with her priestess sisters. This setup would have protected the more advanced souls learning the inner teachings from unwanted and dangerous predators that would persecute them for their instructions. Unfortunately, Peter was too connected to his patriarchal Jewish traditions and noted by other male disciples as stubborn, hot-tempered and quick to anger. He could not grasp these inner teachings and certainly would not have allowed a rival female disciple to be his equal after the resurrection.

Peter's anger and diminishing of Mary and females have been captured in the Pistis Sophia, The Gospels of Mary, Dialogue with the Saviour and other gnostic texts. Jesus is commending Mary on her hard work and dedication to her spiritual path when Simon Peter becomes annoyed that Mary is continually the central figure in these conversations and tells Jesus, "My master, we cannot endure this woman who gets in our way and does not let any of us speak, though she talks all the time."[43] Mary later speaks with Jesus regarding Peter's treatment of her and his apparent dislike of the female race; "My master, I understand in my mind that I can come forward at any time to interpret what Pistis Sophia has said, but I am afraid of Peter because he threatens me and hates our gender."[44] Cleary, Mary is an avid student, asking many questions and learning as much as possible. Peter's jealousy of Jesus and Mary's unique relationship that they converse effortlessly in many texts is glaring. It is apparent why she was shunned so quickly after the disciples separated. Peter feared her authority and understanding of the teachings, a mere woman.

Thus, the world has been led by an incomplete version of the Christian story, a misunderstood story. Until recent years, we have proven that it was dangerous to speak about, much less practice, the gnostic side of the teachings for fear of persecution and death. The Dead Sea findings, Qumran and Nag Hammadi are likely only a small portion of missing texts. It is entirely plausible that many ancient writings are still hidden until humanity is ready to find them. Alternatively, we will raise our consciousness and live from our light beings, and the scrolls from the past will be released, and a new world of ascended beings is our future.

---

[43] Meyer, M. W., Pagels, E. H., Robinson, J. M., Funk, W., & Poirier, P. (2009). *The Nag Hammadi Scriptures: The Revised and Updated Translation of Sacred Gnostic Texts Complete in One Volume* (1st ed.). HarperOne.(Pistis Sophia, 36).

[44] Ibid:43. (Pistis Sophia, 72).

PART 2

THE SEVEN GUARDIANS
RELEASING OUR
ATTACHMENTS
TO THE EGO

CHAPTER 8

THE FIRST BOUGH –
LOVE AND COMPASSION

Release Judgement and Wrath

"And saw the first great bough that bears the
fruit of love and compassion, the foundation
of all things. And I knew that before you can
eat of this fruit and gain its nourishment, you
must be free of all judgement and wrath."[45]

AT THE FIRST BOUGH, YESHUA IS GUIDING MIRYAM TO CONTINUE to ascend her soul to become a "Completion to Completions." To realize ourselves as a divine-human, we must have a solid foundation. We must trust, have faith and a deep knowing that Spirit always loves us no matter the circumstances. The word often placed before love is unconditional. This word suggests that there is an opposite and creates judgement, whether or what is worthy of unconditional love? Infinite love has no opposite; it is all-inclusive, and we do not have to do anything to earn it. In the crucifixion story, we have been told for 2,000 years; Jesus died for our sins. This has created entire societies from generation to generation living in shame and guilt, believing we are not worthy of Divine love. We must continually atone for these sins

---

[45] Quillan, D. J. (2010). *The Gospel of the Beloved Companion: The Complete Gospel of Mary Magdalene*. CreateSpace Independent Publishing Platform. 42:6 (page 117)

that we are born with; the Church has used the crucifixion story for two millennia to maintain control of the people. Guilt is a detractor from the ascension process as it stops the flow of energy and stagnates our evolution. We often pray to "God" to forgive our sins in fear that "he" may punish us or take something away from us for not being perfect. When we judge a situation as "bad,"; it must be because we did something wrong, and God used his wrath to punish us. We often cry out, "God, why has this happened to me; what have I done to deserve this?" This is the first step, the hardest and yet the most basic; releasing judgement and practicing non-attachment to everything. Spirit does not punish us; every experience in this physical realm is an opportunity for us to evolve; it is the whole point of being human, to experience every aspect of what is meant to be human, including the ego. When we become rooted in Divine love, we accept every experience as an opportunity to return to love continually. As Jesus says in the New Testament, it is easy to love your friends and family. In today's society, love is mainly used for the people closest to us. Love comes with expectations, and if you treat me this way, I will continue to love you. This passage's love is our being's true nature; we are love, created by love. It is unity consciousness, loving all of the earth and its beings as One. As we grow and maintain our love of Spirit, recognize the divine in ourselves and all things, we see a reflection of this in all. In Buddhism, love and compassion are the same; they are a state of being. Yeshua loved all things, but as an actual human, he also had a particular fondness for Miryam; he loved her above all women. His state of being was love and compassion for all living creatures, but he had a more intimate relationship with Miryam; this shows us his very human nature. Inviting the Divine into a personal connection, spiritually igniting our sexual energy is the ultimate spiritual transfiguration. Divine love is all-inclusive, and we are the created life from this source, as are all Earth creatures and Mother Earth herself. A famous Eckhart Tolle quote comes to mind "To love is to recognize yourself in another."

Ascension in this passage is not in the hierarchical sense of a vertical ladder going upwards to the kingdom, as in the images of Jacob's ladder. Ascend here refers to drawing all of our consciousness into our heart; the farther we go inward, the higher we go up. Anger or wrath is not good or bad; it is often a nudge that something is not right; we have treated ourselves or have allowed others to treat us as unequal. Wrath alerts us that boundaries have been crossed. When we are enraged, we will say or do things that we will regret if we react from the ego and allow this guardian to have power. The sacred aspect of wrath is an opportunity for us to retreat inward, feel the rage in its entirety, become conscious of what it is trying to show us and feel it fully. Instead of bypassing it or letting it take us over, we allow it to be touched and validated and then allow the soul to inform us of the best action to take that will not harm ourselves or others. We can embrace the wrath, enable it to notify us and then let it go, not resist it, but also do not cling to it. When our masculine and feminine natures are out of balance, the wrath can present itself in a toxic way; masculine: domination or control and in the feminine: unbridled rage or manipulation. The path Yeshua taught, the kenotic path, or the path of self-emptying, is the way to feel fully into our human emotions and feelings. We send love to where we feel the darkness and then release it to the soul, so we make conscious decisions and take action informed by the soul, not reactions from our ego. One of the greatest afflictions affecting our society today is grown-ups who have never faced their childhood traumas; we then pass this on to the next generation. We were taught to suppress our rage and not express anger; shamed to believe our anger was unacceptable. I spent many hours in my bedroom as a child, sent there because I yelled, screamed, and most certainly had temper tantrums.

I could not process where my frustration was coming from, and honestly, I was never asked. I was told it would not be tolerated, and I could stay in my room until I cooled down. Suppressing anger also happened in our schools; we were sent to the corner, the principal's office or in high school, "Room 101." Anger and wrath were not considered appropriate behaviour. I recently watched a movie, "Wisdom of Trauma," led by a Canadian physician Dr. Gabor Mate. The film explained that childhood trauma leads to addiction, imprisonment, mental illness, and a host of diseases in the body. Not being able to express anger leads to wrath, which leads to sickness or endangering ourselves and others. As a society, we have to start inquiring about our children when they act out in rage, what is happening within them, what brought on these emotions, validate them and help them to understand that the anger is not bad. Suppose we can guide them into processing what triggered the outrage, help them work through the event and show them how to transform the emotion with understanding. In that case, we will raise a society capable of communicating the hurt lovingly. As a child, I did not learn how to express or transform the anger, which has led to me avoiding conflict, setting boundaries or vocalizing when someone has hurt me.

In the Gospel of Mary Magdalene, one of the climates described is "lethal jealousy." This type of jealousy is the result of exclusive possession, the attachment to the belief that I own a person, place or thing. If we believe in the laws of the Universe, cause and effect, our actions create consequences, and wrath is often associated with the illusion we own anything in this world. How many murders, predominantly of women, have been attributed to this possessiveness? In North America, almost all domestic violence and murder of women is committed by a jealous husband or boyfriend. When they cannot control their anger in a moment of wrath, the woman has become an object, their possession. We can also look throughout history and see that all wars are because of lethal jealousy, which led to outrage, again, the unchecked rage that justifies us in committing heinous crimes against humanity. All wars started due to believing we have the right to own and conquer people, places or things. We have lost our connection with one another and our Creator in our illusion that this temporary world is ours to own and beat. Everything exists only because of our Divine Mother/Father. As Rumi put it, "I searched for the self, I found God, and I searched for God, I found the self. In finding our true Self, we find God, and in God, we find our true Self".

We are all equal and loved deeply by Spirit, and as we live this love that comes from deep within us, compassion for those not living their authentic truth swells within our soul. Compassion is depicted as a superiority complex in the ego. When we understand that all suffering is a construct of the ego and unnecessary, we can continue to return to our hearts and see what parts need more love. Our fellow humans are not our neighbours; they are us. If anything in this earthly realm is suffering, humans, four-legged, Gaia, we collectively suffer. Someone can only achieve compassion for our own and the world's suffering through the release of judgement and wrath. If we no longer see ourselves as separate, we no longer live in the illusion. If we judge ourselves and others, we also judge Spirit and disconnect from our true nature of love. We see in the other what we see in Spirit, reflecting ourselves, judgement is often a fear or insecurity within us that we project onto others. Spirit only loves; we cannot be anything else. To live in awareness each time the power of judgment or wrath is creeping in is an opportunity for us to return to love and ask ourselves where we are out of alignment. A quote from Marianne Williamson explains this so eloquently; "Just like a sunbeam cannot separate itself from the sun, and a wave cannot separate itself from the ocean, we cannot separate ourselves from one another. We are all part of a vast sea of love, one indivisible divine mind."

The canonical New Testament gospels portray similar teachings, but their true meaning has been lost, "I am the way and the truth and life."[46] Jesus uses the phrase ``I AM`` several times. We also recall in the Old Testament that when God spoke to Moses through the burning bush and Moses questions what name shall he tell the Israelites, God responds with "I AM who I AM, and he said Thus you shall say to the children of Israel I AM has sent me to you."[47] God also tells Moses that the I AM presence is always with him. In both the Old and New Testaments, the church has taught that this is outside of us; it is God or Jesus who are the I am. If the emphasis is intended on I AM, the message is that the Divine presence is all of creation. We are all I AM. We are guided to look within our higher self, the kingdom of heaven within us and each other, the love we are.

The Gospels of Thomas share a great message from Jesus; "If you bring forth what is within you, what you bring forth will save you. If you do not bring forth what is within you, what you do not bring

---

[46] Haynes, C. L., Jr, Haynes, C. L., Jr, Baker, L. L., & Danzey, E. (n.d.). *The Bible - Read and Study Free Online*. Bible Study Tools. Retrieved January 5, 2021, from https://www.biblestudytools.com/John 14:6 KJV

[47] Ibid. KJV Exodus 3:14-15

forth will destroy you."[48] When we come to know ourselves at the deepest level, gnosis, through insightful, intuitive knowledge, love and compassion are our true nature. Judgement and wrath are unknown in the kingdom; these are constructs of the egoic mind, our temporary physical existence. In Adam and Eve's fall, they believed that they were separate and disobeyed God, they were then clothed in humanity, and their eternal selves are hidden inside the body. Yeshua and Miryam came to show us what we forgot and remind us of our natural state of love. Release the attachments and identifications of this false egoic self, peel away the layers of our physical forms and realize we come from the infinite nothingness; we are children of light. Awareness grows each time we recognize who is in charge, the ego or the soul? When we choose the soul as our guide, our decisions and treatment of others are authentic and mirror how the Spirit moves through each of us. We can have compassion for ourselves and others caught in the illusion of suffering and become teachers and guides to help humanity evolve. I AM you, and you are me; there is no duality, only unity. Yeshua said in the Gospel of Philip Verse 57, "Blessed are those who are before coming into being, for those who are, were and will be."[49] We have, will and always will exist in the Oneness before and after our physical matter returns to the Earth.

Judgement creates separation; as we look at the differences in others, we live in the illusion that one is better than the other. When we judge ourselves or others because we allow the guardian at the first bough to have power over us, we are triggered by our own or someone's ego, which binds us to this guardian. We judge our bodies, our thoughts, our emotions based on false interpretations integrated by generations of unaware humans creating from their ego. Lack, scarcity, incompleteness, unworthiness have all been ingrained in our subconscious for centuries. We carry the pain and shame of our ancestors within our DNA. To control the masses, the message instilled

---

[48] Meyer, M. W., Pagels, E. H., Robinson, J. M., Funk, W., & Poirier, P. (2009). *The Nag Hammadi Scriptures: The Revised and Updated Translation of Sacred Gnostic Texts Complete in One Volume* (1st ed.). HarperOne. (The Gospel of Thomas, Saying 114).

[49] Ibid. (The Gospel of Phillip verse 57).

in us is that we were not good enough; we always felt inadequate and not entirely worthy of God's goodness; the Son of God had to be brutally killed to save us, immoral humans. The church suppressed the ascension process and the ability to perform miracles. Yeshua taught us through his example that miracles are our natural state. Once again, the church's crucifixion story that Jesus died for our mortal sins was to instill humanity with guilt so deep that it stagnates our evolution by stopping the flow of energy. Ascension is about becoming conscious of every thought or action; when obstacles arise, they show us where we are out of alignment with our truth, our higher consciousness. Emotions are an awareness of what works for us, not our identity. Wrath or anger shows us that we are out of alignment with what we are creating in our reality. We must retreat in silence and ask ourselves, "Where am I not remembering my oneness?" Guilt is the awareness that perhaps we did not show up for a situation to our fullest potential; we missed the mark. When we identify with guilt, we create judgment; I am unworthy, not good enough, not smart enough. Detachment from our emotions lets us explore where we slid out of alignment and restore our connection with our soul. We chose to have this physical experience in a body as infinite beings for humanity to evolve. As we remember our oneness with Spirit and each other, we begin to fulfill this enormous task. Each time we emanate from the energy of love, we infuse this energy out into the universe. It changes the biological status of every living thing, raises human consciousness, and allows us just to be, which is the nature of what love is.

In the Gospel of Mary Magdalene, "This is why the Good has come into your midst. It acts together with the elements of your nature so as to reunite it with its roots."[50] (Mary 7:20-22). Inside of us, where love dwells, the Good or Spirit merges with our ego to experience life in flow with Divine guidance in the deepest part of us. When we can no longer suffer our lack, our emptiness, our aloneness, we surrender, and the grace of Spirit can fill us and remind us of our "roots" as children of an abundant Universe. Until we are open to receive Spirit's grace, we continue to act from this scarcity mindset.

---

[50] Leloup, J., Rowe, J., & Needleman, J. (2002). *The Gospel of Mary Magdalene* (First Paperback Edition). Inner Traditions. (Mary 7:20-22 Page 55)

Judgement and wrath are emotions associated with this. We live in separateness and look to others as having more or less than us. Any crime of theft or murder stems from believing the other has something we want but lack.

Begin by looking beyond the physical, look deeper, see one another's soul. The patriarchal religions teach about love and compassion in Jesus and then speak of a wrathful male god who will punish those who will not conform. I have been judged for my beliefs and warned that I could choose Heaven (be a believer) or Hell (a non-believer). As a child, it was difficult for me to understand this duplicity. I lived in fear that every action I took could lead to this punishing god sending me to hell or striking me with lightning. However, the deeper we go within and send the energy of love to all of our fears, doubts, negative emotions, we feel the truth of our creator, who loves us unequivocally, every part of us. She does not judge us when we transgress nor punish us; she is not wrathful but invites us, again and again, to return to the heart, encounter what has surfaced and find more ways to send love. Each time the guardian of judgement or wrath invades our thoughts is another opportunity for us to practice love and compassion, to become aware in every moment when this power of the ego is in charge and learn from the experience how we can grow and evolve by facing the darkness and loving it for what it is teaching us at the moment.

Practice love and compassion for everyone you come into contact with, including the beauty of this world. Connect with Mother Earth and nature whenever you feel bound by judgement or wrath. Sit quietly on the ground and go within, dive deep into the darkness; I promise that when you resurface, you will have more peace and harmony. My morning practice is to spend 20 minutes walking barefoot on the grass and putting my hand on each tree in my yard; I tell the tree that I am so grateful for all it provides; oxygen, shelter from the sun. We have one tree that appeared dead in the Spring; within one month of showing it love and gratitude, one-half of the tree sprouted new leaves. I joke with my family that this is our "money" tree; we create miracles with enough faith and trust. This tree provides a resting place for the Blue Jays and other species and gives lovingly without asking for anything in return. We are all love embodied.

Root Chakra – Connection to Mother Earth, body, mind, and soul are grounded and pure

The base or root (muldahara) chakra, located at the base of the spine, governs survival, stability and security. It is related to the first bough as it is the one most securely rooted in our physical existence; our past experiences and memories. Trauma or difficult early life situations can block the energy in this chakra so that we live in fight or flight mode at all times, living in fear in our physical bodies. Yeshua asks us not to be concerned with our physical bodies or even our gender for that matter as it has nothing to do with our true nature. Many scholars were irritated when the Gospel of Thomas was first made public when "Simon Peter said to them: Let Mariham go out from among us, for women are not worthy of life. Jesus said, "Look, I will lead that I may make her male, in order that she too may become a living spirit resembling you males. For every woman who makes herself male will enter into the kingdom of Heaven."[51] We have so many parables where it appears Yeshua is making fun of the disciples for their lack of understanding. In this particular one, along with others, he explains that to enter the kingdom within; gender is irrelevant; our Divine nature does not have a gender; release judgment of the physical's slightest attachment. Forgive and release the past and live in this moment and you will find everlasting joy and peace. Love, compassion and forgiveness greatly enhance our vibrant health. When our energy moves downward in this chakra, we are obsessed with material things and are greedy or insecure. When our life force moves upwards in this chakra, we have a healthy balance with our relationship to material things; we know it is not our eternal home. The colour associated with this chakra is red, the colour of love with a 430–480 THz vibrational frequency.

---

[51] Meyer, M. W., Pagels, E. H., Robinson, J. M., Funk, W., & Poirier, P. (2009). *The Nag Hammadi Scriptures: The Revised and Updated Translation of Sacred Gnostic Texts Complete in One Volume* (1st ed.). HarperOne. Gospel of Thomas Saying 114

My Soul Speaks

The power is within you, believe. I asked for a teacher to come; Spirit replied, "You are the teacher; your story is not about the words or the language, it is the message. Spread love everywhere you go; send love all over the Universe. A bright light embraced me, and she whispered, "I am you, and you are me. I am the saviour I have been waiting for."

Affirmation

Love is my true nature. I am only love.

"You will not be punished for your anger; you will be punished by your anger." Buddha

Exercise - Judgement

Become aware of your thoughts. How do you judge yourself, both physically and emotionally? Each time you notice yourself judging something or someone, practice seeing it through the lens of love. Is there someone you are holding a grudge against? Or a past mistake you made? Can you have compassion knowing they or you did your best at the moment? Send loving thoughts and forgiveness.

Exercise – Wrath

Close your eyes and take three deep breaths; each breath goes deeper within. Then, feel into the anger and rage and ask it to inform you what action needs to be taken from your soul.

When you open your eyes, you can try one of these exercises:

- Write a letter to the person explaining how they hurt you (you will not send the letter) and what made you feel enraged; this letter may even be to yourself – do not judge yourself, feel into your humanity at the moment

- Go outside and scream it out, allow the anger to be released to Mother. She can take it. Scream, cry, feel into it thoroughly and then let it go.

CHAPTER 9

THE SECOND BOUGH – WISDOM AND UNDERSTANDING

Release Ignorance and Intolerance

"The second great bough, weighed down with the fruit of wisdom and understanding, and I saw that before you can taste of its bounty, you must be free of all ignorance and intolerance."[52]

THE FEMININE ASPECT OF GOD IS NAMED SOPHIA, TRANSLATED from Greek to mean wisdom. She is the Mother who births life into the world. In many apocryphal gospels, Sophia is the reason for humanity's fall from grace, not Adam and Eve. The story relates to the human intellect; when we rely on our false wisdom, we remain ignorant of our divine nature without the guidance of proper knowledge from Divine grace. Many early Christian texts suggest that the feminine creates and the masculine puts these thoughts into action. In the Nag Hammadi Scriptures, The Wisdom of Jesus Christ, Jesus says: "The companion of the immortal Human is the great Sophia, who from the beginning was destined to be united with him, by the self-conceived Father, through the immortal Human who appeared as

---

[52] Quillan, D. J. (2010). *The Gospel of the Beloved Companion: The Complete Gospel of Mary Magdalene.* CreateSpace Independent Publishing Platform. 42:7 (page 117)

the first one and as divinity and kingdom."[53] (100, 24). As we begin to see with the heart that all beings are mirrors of Spirit and us, the veils of ignorance and intolerance begin to lift. Ignorance is a lack of knowledge (gnosis); when you live from within and allow your I AM presence to guide your every word and action, great insight and wisdom are bestowed upon you.

As the awareness of our eternal self awakens, it is impossible to return to the illusions of our false egoic identity. Ego identifies with the aspects of our personalities we have acquired, often building walls around our hearts and closing us off to love. Ignorance is described as unawareness; we often choose to remain in this state, unwilling to look at what is happening in our world, our communities, and our own lives; this is called willful ignorance. This choice is because we have refused to grow up and take action on the many ecological, socio-economic and political injustices facing our brothers and sisters worldwide. We can say, "We didn't know," and continue in our tiny bubbles of unconsciousness. Unfortunately, humans have been living in this ignorant state for so long; we are now in a state of emergency. The generations who come after us have an enormous task of cleaning up their ancestors' mess. In Canada, the discovery of hundreds of unmarked graves at the Residential schools has sent waves of shock throughout our Country. These schools were still utilized even as I started grade school in the 1970s. I knew nothing about them and have been immersed with Indigenous communities for years with lacrosse; no one spoke of the horrors too painful to discuss. This is a very dark time in Canadian history; the pain inflicted on these communities appears irreparable, it is going to be a long road to recovery. Children were wrenched from their parents' arms and forced to give up their names, their way of dressing, their culture to become more like the white man. On June 30th, local radio stations collaborated with the Downeywenjack foundation and invited Indigenous leaders, residential school survivors, musicians, and artists to share their stories. I cried the entire day as each one poured their heart out for us to listen. As a privileged white woman, I felt a

---

[53] Parrott, D.M., ed. *Nag Hammadi Codices III,3–4 and V,1 with Papyrus Berolinensis 8502,3 and Oxyrhynchus Papyrus 1081: Eugnostos and the Sophia of Jesus Christ.* NHS 27. Leiden/New York: Brill, 1191 (100, 24)

deep shame that my peoples' ignorance and intolerance invoked them to think they could "fix" or change another culture. The children who did not conform were beaten, raped, and the proof spoken now from the graves, murdered. At its most dangerous, the power of ignorance and intolerance shows when we have completely lost our connection with our oneness, living entirely from the ego. I have heard many say it was not their ancestors who committed these inhumane crimes, but if we are all a part of one universe, then yes, our white ancestors are responsible. My family came to Canada from the United Kingdom in the late 1960s, but we did nothing to try and understand the hardships facing our Indigenous brothers and sisters. We most definitely did not try and acknowledge their ways. We were comfortable with them living on their "reserves," and us living freely in our communities, we did not integrate or socialize. I continue to send love and healing to the survivors of the residential schools, the families whose children never returned home to them and the entire community who have suffered generations of the white man's intolerance of their beauty and uniqueness. I honour you as the original keepers of our beautiful land, and I hope we can reconcile. I ask for your forgiveness of my ignorance, of turning away and not being a witness to the injustices inflicted upon your communities since the invasions began hundreds of years ago. I pray we become brothers and sisters in love once again. A memorial on the National Centre for Truth and Reconciliation website lists the children's names, taken away from their families, never to return. There are still children who lost their lives at these schools and are waiting to be found; I pray they find their way home.

We can choose at times to "forget" that we are not only a body and get caught up in this world of materialism. More often than not, this choice leads to pain and suffering for us and all living creatures. Understanding is only in seeking Spirit's will, transforming the whole being from an ego-centred living to an accepting and all-encompassing worldview. When we see each other, soul to soul, we instantly recognize ourselves in the other. "Mary said, "If Christos can appear as a male, then surely Christos can appear as a female. Those who deny holiness in womanhood do not understand holiness in manhood or womanhood but are sorely bound to ignorance. Do not believe the father of lies.

Believe in the Mother Spirit, whose name is the Spirit of Truth and Comforter!"[54] Miryam is speaking of the truth of our eternal selves; if we turn away anyone, male or female, or by race, culture or religion, and tell them they are unholy or unable to achieve Christ's consciousness, we are ignorant. In accepting our oneness with the All, with creation, with Mother Spirit, we come to know the truth and are comforted by her in the knowledge nothing separates us, and we all can become enlightened in this embodiment.

Yeshua was known in early Christianity as Ihidaya in Aramaic, translated as the enlightened one or unified one. Cynthia Bourgeault explains it as "single one" in Aramaic—one who has unified their being and become what we would nowadays call "enlightened."[55] His spiritual practice led him on the path of inner knowledge, and he taught this path to all who were ready. Mary's Gospel and The Gospel of the Beloved Companion are the profound revelations that this path is available to every one of us. We all can become ihidaya if we put in the work of staying conscious and being aware each time the ego is trying to run the show. Wisdom and understanding know that our false ego is self-induced pain and suffering. The misogynist God who inflicts pain and suffering to punish us was a political figure the church fathers introduced to maintain power over their communities. Our Divine Mother/Father only sees our perfection, innocence, and authentic self. Another great lie was that of original sin, which of course, the blame was put solely on the female human Eve; therefore, all women are wicked and sinful. "And Adam was not deceived, but the woman being deceived was in the transgression."[56] (1 Tim. 2:14). Adam and Eve missed the mark when they believed in the false self-separate from one another, the Earth and our Divine parents. When our awareness expands and sheds the garments of this earthly world, our ego, we see an

---

[54] Malachi, T. (2006). *St. Mary Magdalene: The Gnostic Tradition of the Holy Bride (Gnostic (4))* (First Edition). Llewellyn Publications. p. 147

[55] Bourgeault, C. (2017, April 20). *Be Whole Hearted.* Cac.Org. https://cac.org/be-whole-hearted-2017-04-20/ (Last accessed 2021)

[56] Haynes, C. L., Jr, Haynes, C. L., Jr, Baker, L. L., & Danzey, E. (n.d.). *The Bible - Read and Study Free Online.* Bible Study Tools. Retrieved January 5, 2021, from https://www.biblestudytools.com/1 Tim 2:14

incredible vastness, a world of unlimited possibilities. When Yeshua said to his disciples, "And Jesus said unto them, Because of your unbelief: for verily I say unto you, If ye have faith as a grain of mustard seed, ye shall say unto this mountain, Remove hence to yonder place; and it shall remove; and nothing shall be impossible unto you."[57] (Matthew 17:20). When we are enlightened, all the universe is realized as one, all illusions of separation dissolve. Once you have the wisdom of knowing you are source energy with a human experience, you realize your infinite power to create and move mountains.

Wisdom is a way of knowing deeper, wanting only Divine will to guide your life. It is a shift in consciousness from our head-brain to our heart-brain, the centre of our soul, an awareness of the Cosmic Heart. Here, we begin to detach from our personal dramas, enter the awareness, witness self, and search for the truth in all things. We start living truth as our foundation. The intuitive feeling that we get to follow a particular path is wisdom; this is a feminine aspect, one many of the disciples could not understand. The Sophia/Wisdom story of the fall from grace explains that when we try and live our lives without the guidance of the Divine, we are blindly led by false wisdom. True wisdom lies in knowing we are not separate from our Creator, that she wants to guide us. If we look back on our lives until now, our pain and suffering are most likely when we tried to do things independently when we did not go within the heart, ask deep and meaningful questions, and listen for the answers.

When we attain this awareness of who our eternal selves are, we understand intolerance cannot exist on this new Earth. Another's beliefs or behaviour are not different from our own or the great Spirit of love at our core. We practice discernment, limiting the idea of duality, not judging any circumstance, knowing a Divine plan is always at work. Our physical reality in this dense realm shows that, yes, we have arrived in different cultural settings during this time on this earth realm. We have different skin colours; we follow the religions taught us by our families and society. We are not born intolerant; this is taught to us by others living in the illusion. We have witnessed what this illusion has created, war, famine, poverty, the destruction of several cultures and

---

[57] Ibid:56. Matthew 17:20

sexes. In the name of Christ, history is a devastating tale of crusades, inquisitions, witch burnings, the holocaust, and slavery, to name a few. Miryam is guiding us to see through the illusion to our undeniable sameness within. In physical appearance, I am the rarest human species on earth. It is estimated that only 2% of the world's population has red hair and 17% blue eyes. The combination of both drops significantly.

The witch hunts lasted for over 400 years, with Salem's final trial in 1878. The quests allegedly burnt women predominantly as witches across Europe, many redheads. Red hair was often depicted as demonic, sinful (as in Mary Magdalene, the prostitute in many paintings, yet she was most likely a dark-skinned, dark-haired woman from the middle east.) During the Spanish Inquisition, redheads were branded and burned at the stake. During these horrific years, so many redheads were tortured and murdered because their hair colour signified the fires of hell. We cannot change history, but we have to awaken to avoid future atrocities. I recall a vivid dream I had one evening; it was so real that I awoke drenched in sweat and screaming. It woke my husband, and as he tried to calm me down, I explained the message. I had been turned over to the authorities as a witch by the woman who is my biological mother in this lifetime. I felt the presence of this soul deeply within me. I realized that our role in this incarnation as mother and daughter was the opportunity for us to heal our past life's wounds. My husband asked me if I had the feeling that I have always incarnated as a redhead ... we laughed, and I said, "most likely," I guess I enjoy the challenges!

We are currently experiencing a critical time to wake up worldwide. The pandemic has shed light on social injustices globally. The Black Lives Matter movement has caused many of us to pause and look at how removed we are from our true nature. Dark-skinned humans have been denigrated and subjugated for eons. Racially motivated violence has plagued our societies for thousands of years. The Black Lives Matter movement sets in motion a global opportunity for radical social and political change.

Living an enlightened path and expanding our consciousness into the heart-brain or nous is a momentary practice of mindfulness and awareness. Yeshua and Miryam were the most significant examples for us to follow the path of transformation; they lived the heart's way to show all of us what was possible for humanity. They were radical wisdom teachers who presented humankind with a complete upheaval to the patriarchal churches' belief systems and Roman hierarchy of their time. Unfortunately, as we currently know it and was firmly established in the fourth century, the New Testament omitted many of the first Christian's teachings, most predominantly those closest to Yeshua; Mary, Thomas and Phillip. They were not teaching us to follow a righteous path; they were guiding us to the kingdom/queendom within and demonstrating the power every one of us holds as a child of a most loving Creator. The field of oneness is our divine, natural state; our soul's purpose is to awaken to that within. This wisdom is a sacred state inside the heart, a state of being where we receive the grace of Infinite Source. Our purpose is to continually raise our consciousness by shedding our egoic attachment to ignorance and intolerance and preparing our hearts for the divine grace of wisdom and understanding. Miryam expanded her consciousness to receive Infinite Source's grace to become a great spiritual master of the ageless wisdom teachings. It is now time to ascend the second great bough, and if the master of ignorance calls to us, we can turn inward and joyously live in our interconnectedness.

The Sacral Chakra – Love all dimensions
of thyself, flow, and creativity

The sacral (svadhisthana) chakra is related to sexuality, sensuality and desire. Emotional issues such as ignorance or intolerance block this chakra and stagnate the energy. Many of the early church Fathers who the Roman Church canonized were consumed with desire; Saint Augustine and St. Thomas Aquinas were two prominent ones who cast a shadow over females and rendered the entire female race evil and disgusting. It is documented that Saint Augustine was obsessed with sex and therefore announced that original sin was associated with sex and the female race. Unable to accept that females were equal beings led to ignorance and intolerance and the denigration of the female for the next few thousand years. The sacral chakra out of balance or blocked shows up as unbridled desire, objectification and an inability to flow with life.

When our sacral chakra is balanced, it allows us to be creative, birth new ideas and dictates how we harness our sexual power. Its lower form can show up as controlling or manipulating others. As we raise our state of consciousness in this chakra, we positively use our sexual energy and use wisdom and knowledge to keep our emotions in check; and create a world for the highest good of all. The colour associated with this chakra is orange with a 480-510 THz vibrational frequency.

My Soul Speaks

As I sunk deeper into my heart centre, a great Spirit guide appeared. This guide was extremely tall with long flowing hair, warrior-like. I have often seen/felt the presence of a great warrior chief with me. He knelt in front of me and took my hands, and said, "Remember who you are." Over and over again. "All you have to do right now is embody love; remember your oneness, and everything else will fall into place."

Affirmation

My journey to freedom is blessed and sacred. I have come to know the Divine within myself more deeply and profoundly. May that knowing lead to a new openness in my heart. May I be opened to receive and experience love, joy, peace, abundance, satisfaction and wholeness.

Exercise

- Sit quietly with your pen and journal. Take three deep breaths and drop into your heart.
- Ask your soul what area in your life do you live in duality?
- Choose a person from your past or present you have not viewed as your equal – whether superior or inferior. Bring that person into your inner vision and gaze deeply into their eyes. Repeat these words "I am you, and you are me, we are equal and all part of one consciousness."

CHAPTER 10

THE THIRD BOUGH – HONOR AND HUMILITY

Free of Duplicity and Arrogance

"The third great bough, which bears the fruit of
honor and humility. Only when free of all duplicity
and arrogance may you partake of its nourishment."[58]

A S WE REACH THE THIRD BOUGH, WE ARE BEGINNING TO ACCEPT
ourselves as children of a Divine Mother/Father and seeing
the greatness of all creation. When God gave Moses the Ten
Commandments and asked us to honour our mother and father, it was
taught in the literal sense of our biological mother and father. What if
God was revealing the truth of our eternal creators? In the canonical
gospels, Jesus asks his disciples to leave their parents and serve only
Source/God, our true parents, our heavenly mother and father. In this
sense, we cannot see duplicity in any creation in the universe as we all
are part of one large family, united as one. When we awaken to the
deception that we are not separate from one another or any creation, it
is as though a great veil is lifted. The truth of our interconnectedness
with the universe confirms we are and never have been alone. The
illusion no longer binds us to believe in this false sense of separation;

---

[58] Quillan, D. J. (2010). *The Gospel of the Beloved Companion: The Complete Gospel
of Mary Magdalene*. CreateSpace Independent Publishing Platform. 42:8 (page 118)

it was a coming home, a sense of belonging for myself. I sit in silence on the grass and feel my connection with Gaia, with the birds singing, the wind whispering and feel every breath enveloped in the love of my divine parents; a complete sense of peace penetrates my very essence.

The definition of honour is a clear sense of morally right and just, high respect and great esteem. Throughout his ministry, Miryam was always by Yeshua's side in the many apocryphal texts and the canonical gospels. She witnessed the most important events, the crucifixion and the resurrection. Although she is barely mentioned in the New Testament accounts of Jesus' life, she is the first, and sometimes only one, said at the most critical moments. Additionally, she is consistently named first, before all of the other Mary's, except in the Gospel of John. Indicating her pivotal role as the one he loved the most, the disciple who lived a fully human and fully divine life alongside Yeshua; she was his first twin.

In many of the gnostic gospels, Yeshua continually commends Miryam on being blessed for coming into being before coming into being. Her focus and intent are on the Queendom of Heaven within her; these are clear and concise words that tell us everything we need to know about Miryam's state of being, her consciousness. Yeshua commends her for following his teachings so precisely and understanding their meaning. Miryam has realized her queendom within; she has merged her earthly incarnation with her divine spirit, released the ego's desire to see duplicity or separateness and humbly embraces her humanity. In overcoming the ego's deceitfulness of this material world's illusions, we can look into our neighbours' eyes and see our unity. Namaste means "The spirit in me sees the spirit in you." When we greet each other with this word, we recognize ourselves in the other. The ego is crafty in its attempt to deceive us into believing that we are better or less than others; we are different for so many reasons.

I have recently realized that often in our search for meaning and purpose, we arrive at answers sometimes so profound that we want to share the information with everyone. The exciting thing is that we all perceive information in different ways; a crafty ego trick is to create a spiritual superiority in our psyche. I have learned to recognize when my ego speaks, my voice gets an octave louder, my heart beats a little faster, and before I know it, I can be in a heated debate trying to prove my point, often yelling, "God is not a man!" Even though I am sharing what I believe to be a divine revelation, the guardian of arrogance has sneakily crept in, and the lesson is lost; it is no longer coming from my divine self but my egoic head-brain. Our divine nature remains untouchable, unchangeable. Every one of us is perfect, and when we speak and listen from the eye of the heart, we are not attached to an emotion, then we can recognize arrogance when it rears its nasty head. When we live a life in alignment with our true nature, life begins to flow through us, and we are led to live an extraordinary life peacefully with all of creation. Ego wants us to believe we are superior beings, not only to other humans but to all of creation. This is very evident in our hyper-materialistic head-brain thinking. We are so arrogant that we have created a global environmental crisis, global inequality and the extinction of thousands of beautiful creatures. We are also on the brink of extinction ourselves. I recall a story of the Indigenous tribes of North America being confused when the colonials wanted to "buy" land from them. They believe we have been awarded the responsibility to care for all of Earth and its creations; we are all intrinsically connected through Spirit. As you will recall, during one of my meditations, I was guided to listen to the lessons of the Indigenous tribes; they speak of humanity's grand awakening from our slumber, our illusion of believing that we are the superior species. If this awakening does not happen, we will destroy the earth and ourselves with our arrogance; we already see it happening on land, sea and sky.

When we reach the stage of humbly surrendering our will to that of Divine will, we are truly ready to accept all assignments the universe asks of us, however great or small. I recall being deep in prayer and contemplation and asking the Great Spirit to guide me on my path, and then I quietly whispered, "But please do not ask me to build an ark." As I realized how ridiculous this sounded, I could not stop laughing and felt that my divine mother was laughing right alongside me, saying, "Why don't you start again, this time with no expectations?" That evening I shared the experience with my family; we all had a good chuckle imagining me on the farm out back building an ark. My children reminded me that I had planted a burning bush in the garden if "God" wanted to reveal something to any of us. They also call me the crazy lady who speaks to the birds, the trees, all creatures, and yes, I believe they communicate back to me. I was having my morning coffee at the back of our property, and a blackbird was perched upon the feeder; he was calling out to me, I realized the feeder was empty. I came to the house and got the bag of seed to fill it up and heard my husband tell my son that, "Mom is speaking to her birds again; they informed her they needed more food." Years ago, I would have been afraid to reveal my authentic self for fear of being labelled crazy. Now I embrace my eccentricity and am eternally grateful it has opened my family up to search for deeper meaning and accept our oneness with everything.

Each of us is called upon to serve a greater purpose; with humility, we accept the task without hesitation; it is our duty to creation to answer the call. We consciously know that it is a divine plan in motion when we hear the call with greater awareness. Some are asked to perform feats that seem impossible, but as co-creators with Infinite Source, we must humbly accept the call and trust we are never alone; we are always guided and supported. We are equal to all creatures on Earth and as crucial as those in the spiritual world. We are worthy of receiving guidance from all realms. We can call on the support of angels, ascended masters, ancestors; they are waiting to assist us in all matters, especially when answering a call from Spirit. When we are truly humbled, we have no fear of what might be asked of us, and nothing is insignificant. Everything is part of the great Divine plan, and we understand duplicity is an illusion; we are all connected. We must accept our assignments with great honour, grateful to be called. When my middle son was eight years old, he was "cut" from his AA hockey team. He was devastated; how could he possibly go to school the next day and face his friends and teammates? I put my hands on either side of his eyes and explained that this is the limited vision we have; I then removed my hands and held them out as wide as I could and said, "This is what God sees." It is difficult for us when faced with challenging life circumstances because we do not always know the "long game." Jonathan (my son) spent the rest of his hockey years with young men who are now his closest friends; they won many championships together, travelled to tournaments and enjoyed the sport immensely without the pressure the higher level may have put on them. When we surrender to divine will, take each moment with intentional action, we can achieve anything, and as Yeshua tells us, all will be revealed.

The most relevant teaching we can teach our children is humility, but we teach our children about their importance and feed their egos in fear they may not achieve the success we believe is theirs in this lifetime. In our attempt to have "perfect" children, kids better than our friends' offspring, we often create a hostile environment in our homes and deeply traumatize our children unknowingly. This trauma creates an inflated ego, a wall around their hearts that protects them from revealing their authentic selves. They are what the adults around them told them to be, and in this, they feel unworthy at their core. Their dreams of being an artist were thwarted with the demand to earn a six-figure income and show how successful their families are. We have only to look at the massive campaigns against bullying in our school systems to see what we are creating. Unresolved trauma is carried into the corporate world and our governments. Donald Trump is a prime example of the guardian of this ego power, arrogance and duplicity out of control. Honouring one another as equals is one of the things lost as we gradually moved out of communal-based living. I often heard it takes a village to raise a child. Then we became "helicopter" parents, dictating everything our children did and put ourselves and our own families first in a race to be the most successful in the eyes of all others living in the illusion. How often, when parents are asked how the family is, do they begin first by describing their children's material accomplishments, their degrees, elite recognition by an establishment in the patriarchal system? This is the masculine nature that has dictated our lives for thousands of years, strive, do, push. The feminine energy allows, receives, is guided by intuition. The key is balance, allowing ourselves to be guided by our divine spark (feminine) and then creating with action (masculine) the life we were called to live in this incarnation. I began my university career as a theatre major with a minor in English, and I was thriving, immersed in Shakespeare, poetry, screenplays; it was glorious for three years. In my third year, the question was raised about what type of career could I possibly pursue with a degree in theatre studies? Doubt had been seeded, I switched to psychology, spent my year miserable and at the end of it, the University went on strike for months. I fled to London, England, to "find myself" and never ended up with a degree. I did attempt to return after my eldest son was born, taking distance learning courses, and amazingly, another strike halted my progression. As I look back, I changed who I was and what I was passionate about to fit into a society that demanded we pursue careers based on monetary value and perceived success instead of humbly accepting my unique gifts of creativity.

One of our local high schools used to have an exchange program with a school in Nunavut, Canada's newest and most Northern province, land of the Inuit, an Indigenous people, whom the United States refer to as Eskimos. The program was cancelled because when the Inuit youth would return to their homes, they were rebellious and dissatisfied with their village life. When in town, they stayed in homes five times the size of their own, with several big-screen televisions and what they perceived as prosperous life. They were ashamed of their homes, and when the exchange reversed, they did not want these superior Southern youth to see where they lived. I knew the local school secretary, and when she explained their lifestyle, it sounded beautiful. When she supervised one trip during a summer month, the community experienced twenty-four hours of daylight; toddlers could ride their bikes at four in the morning, the entire village gathered and danced into the wee hours. Each member of the community looked out for one another. The exchange created an inferiority complex in their youth, and many, when they were able, wanted to move South to live what they perceived to be a better lifestyle.

If we lived in communities where every child is raised to know and value every living thing's importance, as above, so below and equal, the next generation may eradicate the crises plaguing our world today, both environmental and social. If we taught meditation and dropped into our heart centre in schools instead of politics and a skewed history written by the white man, could we also alleviate all bullying? That is hell, yes! When we become aware that we are all connected, we will respect the Earth. I am equal to the birds in the sky, the fish in the oceans, my fellow humans, the spirit world. Our importance greatly diminishes when we see the greatness in the Universe, from the tiniest bug to the grand giraffe, so intricately created in such magnificent detail. We must learn to care for Mother Earth as she has watched and provided for us since the beginning of time. Pollution will cease, overconsumption and greed would no longer be even a thought in our minds. The recent pandemic has shown us how caught up we are in our self-importance; the toilet paper crisis will, I am certain, have future enlightened generations shaking their heads at us. Many hoarded, grocery shelves were empty of pantry staples, families left the shops with three, sometimes four grocery carts, afraid they would not survive, not caring for their neighbours. The self-preservation witnessed is entirely operating from the ego, forgetting we have a powerful Creator, having faith and trust that all our needs are always met. With humility, free of duplicity, poverty would no longer be an issue because we would not spend trillions of dollars on military or weapons of war. We would not have to build walls or even borders to keep "others" out. There would be no others, only one, working our uniqueness into the whole. In Matthew 5:5, Jesus says, "Blessed are the meek for they will inherit the Earth."[59] This Beatitude informs us of our purpose on this Earth; to be in service to each other and all things. To be in service, we must do two things, not inflate our own identity or think more highly of ourselves than others and accept our strengths and abilities as an opportunity to use whatever powers were bestowed upon us in service to others. This is a beatitude of becoming humble and surrendering, allowing the divine to act through us and all of creation.

I love the story of the Liverpool soccer player Sadio Mane who has become a world-renowned player. Mane is a wealthy and successful man because of his Divine given talents. However, he is also a humble servant, providing funds to his poverty-stricken homeland of Bambali Senegal. He has helped build a hospital, a secondary school and donated thousands of British pounds to relieve the poverty of his people. He regularly sends money to the families in his hometown to live a reasonably decent life. A few videos went viral, showing him arriving at his local mosque in Liverpool and cleaning the toilets. A BBC article

---

[59] Haynes, C. L., Jr, Haynes, C. L., Jr, Baker, L. L., & Danzey, E. (n.d.). *The Bible - Read and Study Free Online*. Bible Study Tools. Retrieved January 5, 2021, from https://www.biblestudytools.com/Matthew 5:5

wrote this about him, "He's not a person looking for fanfare. There's no arrogance." This humility is evident in several stories about Mane."[60] He has been gifted the powers to become a rich and famous footballer and uses those powers in service to those less fortunate humbly.

A Course in Miracles states: "All the Children of God are special and none of the children of God are special."[61] We each have unique gifts and talents. These are meant to be shared in a glorious, joyous dance. The Divine loves us equally and is delighted with life just for the sheer love for all of creation. We are meant to create with each other, for each other and only for the pleasure of sharing our divine gifts. It was clear from a very young age that I was never going to be a mathematician or a rocket scientist, but I was creative and loved to write and act on stage to entertain others. When we got together with our extended families, I would have a play written each Christmas. My siblings and cousins would perform the play after dinner for our parents. In grade eight English class, I wrote a Christmas play called Fire and Ice. It was chosen to be the holidays' performance, presented to the entire school and our families. I was one of the leads (Fire princess) and helped direct it. These were my gifts to the world, but I allowed false teachings to be ingrained in my ego and, based on fears of unworthiness or not smart enough, allowed these powers to move into the background. As I realized my true nature, when the fears start to arise, I now recognize my ego, go deep into my heart centre and clear any blocks or obstacles of false identity. I know I am good enough and intelligent enough.

---

[60] Hancock, Adam (November 26, 2018) Liverpool's Sadio Mane: 'He has a Bentley at home but drives to the mosque in a not-so-fancy car' - BBC Sport

[61] Foundation For Inner Peace. (1992). *A Course in Miracles, Combined Volume: Text, Workbook for Students, Manual for Teachers, 2nd Edition* (2nd ed.). Foundation for Inner Peace.

Solar Plexus Chakra – My will and Divine will are one. I quickly manifest from my connection to the abundant universal flow.

The solar plexus chakra (Manipura) represents our power. The colour associated with this chakra is orange with a 510-540 THz vibrational frequency. If this chakra flows downwards, it can cause a desire for power for our own selfish purpose. As we move this upwards, we use our power in service to others; we are self-empowered and know that we also help ourselves and create by assisting others and being in service to humanity. We merge our will with divine will, and life flows through us; we do not have to strive; we naturally become. We manifest everything life offers because we are deeply connected with the universal flow. As a result, we live in honour and humility, leaving behind arrogance and duplicity.

My Soul Speaks

As I drew my energy through the deep rich soil, past all the tree roots and rock deep to the centre of the Earth, I encountered the most loving energy. This energy was a startling sapphire avatar that drew me to her bosom. As I lay my burdens on her lap, I began to feel radiating ruby energy surround us. There was an immense feeling of unconditional love. A love so all-encompassing, I knew I was united in the trinity of Mother/Father/Child, and I was safe in their embrace. When I returned to my body, I knew that I was love and nothing else in my entire being.

Affirmation

I am humbled when I look at the beauty that surrounds me. I thank Infinite Source for trusting me, breathing life into me and allowing me to live this human life. I ask each day for guidance on serving for the greatest good of all. I do a small part each day to love and protect the Earth and my fellow humans; we are all in this together. I know, Spirit intensely loves us, simple humans, even when we forget our Divine lineage.

Exercise

Being human is a gift from the divine; many gifts and talents are evident to the head-brain. For example, some of us are naturally athletic, creative, intelligent. But, unfortunately, many of our soul gifts are deeply buried from past trauma, and we are afraid to have them manifest in our physical reality.

Sit quietly and take deep breaths, each time dropping deeper into your heart centre. Then, with your pen and journal close by, ask your soul to reveal your gifts or talents that have yet to be realized to you or have been long forgotten, buried beneath your fears and doubts. When you are ready, gently open your eyes and write in long-hand for at least ten minutes. This exercise may take several practices to reveal your deeper reality and potential; your lost and forgotten gifts will begin to appear upon the pages.

CHAPTER 11

FOURTH BOUGH – STRENGTH AND COURAGE

Weakness of the Flesh – Conquer the illusion of your fears

"The fourth bough, blossoming with the fruit of
strength and courage. And I heard him tell me that
to eat of this fruit, you must have freed yourself
from the weakness of the flesh and confronted
and conquered the illusion of your fears."[62]

W E ARE EASILY DISTRACTED BY OUR BODIES' PHYSICAL NEEDS,
our bodies have strong desires, and our desires tempt us.
In this sense, desire refers to egoic desire, craving, and
what our head-brain thinks we know, want, or need to have. A desire
that comes from the ego never satisfies us; once we get that next
thing, its appeal wears off, and we are constantly looking for the next
something to fulfill us. We are no longer living in the present moment;
we compare our past and want more things than we had yesterday for
our future. Our body's needs and the material world are not bad or
wrong (we have already moved through the bough of judgement). We
have desires for us to survive in this earthly realm. Sexual desire can

---

[62] Quillan, D. J. (2010). *The Gospel of the Beloved Companion: The Complete Gospel
of Mary Magdalene.* CreateSpace Independent Publishing Platform. 42:5 (page 117)

lead us on a path of spiritual bliss and procreation, cocreating with the Divine bringing forth new life.

Eating is necessary for our body temples to function at optimum capacity. When we overindulge our earthly desires, we move into lower morality decisions of jealousy, greed, anger, and hatred. We develop negative habits, personal vices, and a distraction from our more incredible spiritual path. We allow the material world to take precedence over our more profound inner soul nature, our true soul desires. The only way to renounce the lower desires that lead to immediate personal gratification is surrender. When we can no longer resist the pull of ego desire wanting more, needing more, the only way out is in. We fall to our knees, and we pray, and then we listen through meditation, connecting with our inner divine guidance and asking what action to take for the greatest good of all. When this guidance leads us, we have the strength and fortification to transform our earthly personal desires into divine desires. As we stay in awareness of the physical nature of the body, taking care of its needs, honouring it with the essentials to run smoothly, resist unhealthy cravings, we allow our body to become a vehicle of consciousness. The flesh (body) is temporary, will pass away, return to the earth at the hour of our death. The Master of the world, the ego, will continually try and pull us back into the world of the five senses. To live a pure life in Spirit, we must release the illusion that the material realm is our master.

In its attempt to minimize Christ's humanity and portray him as more "Godly," the Church created an image of an idol that society could never be like in this lifetime. This included physical intimacy or sex, which was far too human for their new "Godhead" ever to have engaged in, so they stripped away his humanity and created a false portrayal of a celibate Jesus. Miryam disappeared into the background, her role as his partner and co-minister obscured from history. I recently saw a cartoon of a monk whose duty each day was to descend to the monastery's basement for hours each day, translating scripture. One day, he did not resurface at dark, so the other monks searched for him. They found him at the desk over a papyrus crying; the other monks were concerned and asked him what was wrong. He looked up and said, "He didn't say celibate; he said celebrate."

Until the fourth century, the first Christians (Nazarenes) taught and practiced that we are all equal, which is why they were persecuted and killed. They were directly connected with Spirit and spoke of no other authority for their lives; this was treason, no one was above Caesar, and those who suggested this, were crucified. They also preached that everyone, men, women, and slaves, is brothers and sisters, equals. When Constantine and his gathering of all male clergy met at the council of Nicea to debate whether they were going to present Jesus as a man enlightened or God come to earth (the priests who agreed on the former were quietly removed from the vote), they also created a hierarchy within the church that excluded women from any leadership roles. This also strengthened their resolve that women on the scale rank right down at the bottom with slaves. When editing the disciples' stories, choosing which books to include in the New Testament, the council decided that women would not be a part of the Christian story. Hence, a Virgin/Immaculate Mary and a female sinner became the two archetypes females had as their role models. The originally prominent females amongst the first Christians were afforded little exposure in the New Testament books. I relentlessly questioned the virgin Mary once I was old enough to understand sex and how babies were created. The instruction was to believe the miracle and never disbelieve it. The closest we can come to know the Divine and our role as co-creators is to create a child with our beloved through sacred sexual union. To birth new souls has been the greatest calling of this embodiment for me. They were the most beautiful, joyous moments in my life. To diminish this sacred act and make it wrong or wicked has robbed all of us of our creative power. In a blatant attempt to decrease the feminines' astonishing ability to grow and birth new life, those with their egoic ignorance brandished women as lowly, dirty and replaceable. Of course, Eve's transgressions led to women being punished by having to bleed monthly and endure excruciating pain during childbirth. Here we have our wrathful father once again meting out punishment to the lesser sex. These words were spoken by men of power who could influence thousands. Any woman who has birthed a child will tell you that they barely remember the pain when their child is put into their arms, and we admit we would go through it all again, and the pain is worth the result. The early translation of the word Virgin, dating back to the Goddess days, is Pure of Heart. This explanation of the biological mother of Yeshua resonates with me; when we are virgin, pure of heart, we may come to know the divine within us.

The teaching that the body is dirty, sinful was the exact opposite of the message of Yeshua, Miryam and the first Christians, and they wanted all of us to know the great power we all carry within us to become fully realized humans in this embodiment. Sex is not innately wrong; if it is performed from egoic desire, it has to conquer and have, with no soul involvement, that it becomes a flesh's weakness. When we have an unhealthy identification with the material world and forget that we are also a soul, it leads to sexual addiction, obesity, and a myriad of other illnesses in the body. This also leads us down the slippery slope of bad habits that cannot fulfill our purpose in this lifetime. Debilitating conditions and early bodily death can occur. This same guardian is described in the Gospel of Mary as a zeal for death, not paying attention to our physical body to the point of disease. The denigration of the female body has led to our bodies not belonging to us; given away by Fathers, sold by brothers for centuries. As far as we have come, the female became disposable, and our bodies are still being bought and sold in the often hidden, dark underbelly of human trafficking, mainly in the sex slave industry.

I spoke earlier of a crisis in 2017 that led me deeper into my search for the Goddess in the story of humanity. My daughter, Alexis, is a survivor of human trafficking in the sex industry. The man she believed loved her, exploited her vulnerability and youthful naivety, and sold her body to the highest bidders. The shame and guilt built up within her until she eventually left the world in her mind, which led to psychosis; she left the reality she found herself living in. Psychosis is not an illness; it is a symptom, and in her case, caused by extreme trauma. Alexis spent a month in the hospital and, to this day, still experiences the effects of post-traumatic stress disorder. I questioned myself relentlessly in those early days of this discovery, what had I forgotten to teach her about loving herself? I believed this was my fault, and I had failed as a mother. I had never really studied the Goddess; of course, I knew of the more famous Greek and Egyptian Gods and Goddesses of history; these were vaguely taught in history class. The Goddess Brighid began appearing in my inner vision. Initially, she appeared facing away from me; I could only see her long flowing red hair and gown of deep emerald velvet. At first, I thought it was a younger version of myself coming with a message, something I had forgotten; her visions filled me with a great sense of peace. The first time I saw her face was when I asked for a sign that the path we had chosen to press charges against her trafficker was for Alexis's highest good. I knew that this choice would retraumatize her when we arrived at the trial date, and she would have to be a victim–witness. I turned over Brigit's card from the Goddess Oracle I had recently purchased by Doreen Virtue. I gasped when I saw her face for the first time; her piercing eyes held me in a trance; I held my breath and whispered, "I know you." Her message was so clear, and when I realized why this stunning Goddess was appearing to me, the tears flowed. Her message is, "Stand up for what you believe is right." The full message in the oracle is "Do not back down."[63] It assured me that she was here to help me navigate this uncharted territory, to support and protect me, and in turn, allowing me to be strong for my daughter. As I began searching for more information on Brighid, she remained with me, always guiding me to the next right step in dealing with the judicial system and my girl's fragile and delicate state. Brighid is a Celtic triple Goddess, where my ancestors hailed. She was the only part of pagan Ireland St. Patrick could not destroy when he rid Ireland of the snakes. The serpent is a symbol of the Goddess, representing life and regeneration; the snakes he exterminated were the pagan beliefs in the Goddess. Still, the people would not allow her to be taken from them in Ireland, and by many names and spellings across Europe, so she became Saint Brigit in Christianity. Brighid is the patroness of healing, among others, and with certainty, I knew she was my benefactress for inner healing. In the many months she appeared to me, she reminded me of the sacredness of motherhood, how this is the greatest calling in this lifetime, and that now was not the time to be a passive mother. It

---

[63] Virtue, D. (2004). *Goddess Guidance Oracle Cards* (Box ed.). Hay House Inc.

was time to fight with all my might for my child and the many other children these traffickers had destroyed. Brighid is honoured in her capacity as the Great Mother, and she shares many of the same symbols as Isis, the Egyptian Goddess. The Goddess, I believe the Marys' from the bible studied in her Egyptian temples. As Brighid transitioned from Goddess to Saint in Christianity, a legend sprung that she was the midwife who helped birth the baby Jesus into the physical world. Of course, this is a myth, but it speaks volumes of her important role as Queen of the Heavens, a title later attributed to Mother Mary. Early Celtic tribes were matrilineal; names and lands were passed down through the females. During this time, motherhood was revered as the most important role in a tribe, and mother Goddesses were often depicted as warriors. Rape was the most punishable crime, and Brighid was a fierce warrior defending women's rights. Brighid came to me in my darkest hours, and her guidance helped me rekindle the fire within my heart and remember my role as a fierce mother. The preliminary trial and later sentencing of my daughter's perpetrators were long and gruelling; she was put through hell on the stand, an unfortunate evolution of our patriarchal justice system. The victim is often blamed and degraded in an attempt to win at all costs. Brighid stayed with me through the entire ordeal; she often arrived in my vision with Kuan (Guan) Yin; together, they supported me with their fierce warrior strength and compassion until I had the strength to stand on my own. A year following the trial, my friend Christine had come up for a sleepover; we tend to chat for hours. I had purchased an emerald, green silk blouse and was showing it to her. I never in my life spent $265.00 on a piece of clothing. I explained to her that I wore it every time I wanted to connect with Brighid and explained the story of my visions. Christine's jaw dropped, she proceeded to tell me of a painting she created as a ten-year-old. When she sent me a picture of it the next day, we knowingly smiled; we were destined to be part of one another's soul tribe, Brighid connected us. The image below is a copy she made for me for my birthday; Brighid sits above my altar, protecting our household, with Archangel Michael, her warrior, masculine counterpart.

Painting of Brighid, by Christine Barone

Sexual exploitation of women, young men and children worldwide is another pandemic affecting our society. It is a glaring example of how far we have fallen into ego desires, personal gratification at all costs. The guardian of the ego power, weakness of the flesh, controls the sellers and the buyers of these exploited young people. In her infinite wisdom, Brighid brought me back into my own heart, to the place of love and healing. With her determined strength and courage, my daughter found her voice through this traumatic experience. In going to the police, which led to the arrest and sentencing of six people involved in an organized crime ring, she was not only standing up for herself, but for all women who came before and will come after, she was raising her fist and declaring, "This ends with me!"

Our drives to and from the courthouse were spent with the song "Wild Hearts Can't Be Broken" from Pinks Beautiful Trauma album blaring through the speakers. Alexis later painted a broken Angel, hunched over, covered in cuts and bruises, dressed in black leather lingerie and a ball and chain attached to her foot; the inscriptions in the painting are lyrics from this song. Painting was a critical part of her healing, just as I need meditation; this was her connection with the divine aspect of herself; she connects to her divine nature through the art of painting. Although Pinks's song has no relevance to human trafficking, our interconnectedness is evident in how all artists can transcend their craft to become meaningful in any circumstance.

We also carry the trauma of our ancestors within us; in speaking up and standing up for what she believed in, Alexis was healing generations of trauma inflicted upon the female race, and specifically within her ancestral line. Our ancestors live within us always, and I believe so do the energies of the Goddess, they may have been silenced for a time, but she has never really been gone. Mary Magdalene was labelled a prostitute because of the fear men had for her authority and influence, continuing to grow throughout the Christian world. Her gospels were buried deep in the desert, but their attempt to obliterate her from our hearts was ineffective. I often wonder if The Gospel of the Beloved Companion was what the Cathars and Knights of the Templar so vehemently protected. They were persecuted and killed for their protection of her and her bloodline. Many of the young women I have met who have been sexually exploited cling to Mary Magdalene, the prostitute, as their patron saint. I do not correct their image of her, nor do I give an opinion; if this is the divine feminine who helps their abused and broken hearts to mend, she can be whatever they need; I know Miryam has the strength to hold them. I believe she has the power to guide them into their hearts and show them their worth, bring them back to love, regardless of the egoic label patriarchy attributed to her.

As we ascend our thoughts and feelings into guided intuition from our I AM Presence, we are rewarded with peace, love, joy, selflessness and courage. We must test these daily and maintain a constant spiritual practice of praying and meditating to know the truth of who and what is speaking with us. When a desire overcomes us, it is an opportunity to check in with our bodies. Do I want another glass of wine, or does my body require a cup of tea and an early night? We learn to walk in Spirit and allow life to flow through us; our words and actions reflect this. When we are conscious of the fleshs' weakness and see a life beyond the five senses, remember we are also a soul, we can recognize when the physical body enslaves us. We must strive to develop the strength and courage to listen to our souls' desires. Our soul walks with eternal Spirit.

When we define ourselves by our physical attributes, we limit our experiences. They describe our limited physical existence that is only viewed through the five senses; these definitions keep us from our true, vast nature; they limit us to a set of social norms, which are ever-changing with the times. The descriptions also carry burdens; after 4,000 years of oppression, girls and women bear the trauma of their ancestors and all women who came before them in their DNA. The prophet Muhammad said, "Die before you die," a later version of what Yeshua also taught, die to your ego self. This illusion of separation from Spirit invites us through prayer, devotion and meditation to come home to our true selves and rest in the presence of love. We do not base anything on physical attributes; we look at each other and creation through the heart's eye; here, we are all equal and beautiful. Die to the illusions of the material world and come home. Deny the master of the world and be set free! The Divine captures our hearts when we tune into our souls and feel her presence. The Divine meets us here, in our hearts, to commence direct communication, where we radiate love beyond our plan and allow divine guidance to lead us.

"And I say unto you my friends, Be not afraid of them that kill the body, and after that have no more that they can do"[64] (Luke 12:4). Almost the entire twelfth chapter of Luke in the New Testament speaks directly to fear. In this quote, Jesus informs his disciples not to fear death or their enemies, for once they kill the body, they cannot harm them any further. Once we have recognized the flesh's limitations, we have nothing else to fear. It is important to note here that the only disciple who fully embraced this teaching was Miryam. She never left him through the trial, when Peter denied him, nor the crucifixion when all the male disciples hid; she did not fear her possible persecution. Her intense love of her beloved kept her steadfast for the entire three days up until the resurrection. The other disciples scattered and hid, afraid of death. Mary followed as they carried her beloved's body to the tomb

---

[64] Haynes, C. L., Jr, Haynes, C. L., Jr, Baker, L. L., & Danzey, E. (n.d.). *The Bible - Read and Study Free Online*. Bible Study Tools. Retrieved January 5, 2021, from https://www.biblestudytools.com/Luke 12:4

and arrived with her alabaster jar of spikenard to anoint his physical body in preparation for his Ascension and resurrection of his light body, not fearing the Romans.

Yeshua and Miryam were spiritual guides to lead us on a spiritual path of enlightenment, free from the material world's illusions. Although many of the New Testament books have been edited or redacted over the centuries and incorrect language translations handed down, they have often been misunderstood. Jesus tells them, "Therefore I say unto you, take no thought for your life, what ye shall eat, or what ye shall drink; nor yet for your body, what ye shall put on. Is not the life more than meat, and the body than raiment?."[65] (Luke 12:25-26) Again, Jesus is teaching them about the nature of life and death. We currently live in fear of death because we believe our lives are linear. Birth and Death are not separate; we are cyclical in nature. We are born, die, and are reborn again; we are like waves in the ocean that cannot be separated from our Source. This verse from Luke also informs us that our Creator has a divine plan for each one of us; therefore, we do not have to worry about our life; all will be well. When Yeshua teaches us that the kingdom of heaven is within and is in our midst, he is not referring to a place far away; we must earn the right to enter in the future. He is saying that all of creation is the kingdom of heaven. Our Divine parents are actively involved in our lives, always present within us. In Luke, he imparts this knowledge to his disciples; even if they kill your body, they cannot hurt your true essence, your eternal being. He then tells them; you have nothing to fear; your life is not of this physical being, this vessel.

Additionally, we must have faith and trust that Spirit is always looking out for us; again, the divine plan is constantly in motion, even if we cannot sense it. Miryam cultivated an inner strength to venture ultimately into the world of Spirit while humbly embracing her full humanity. She completely embraced her divine nature with her human nature and overcame the illusion of her fears. She and Yeshua had no interest in the kingdom of this world, for they knew that they were doing light work for a much grander realm than this world, the inner realm of our being, directly connected with Spirit. The most significant blocks on our path to realizing our divine nature are attachments to the

---

[65] Ibid:64. Luke 12:25-26

physical world's illusions. These attachments manifest in many forms from material goods, job status, wealth, and each of these attachments comes from deep-rooted fears. The fear of loneliness can lead us to hold onto a miserable life with someone who mistreats us. The fear of poverty keeps us in jobs that suck the life out of us. Our fears manifest in our physical reality and cause pain and suffering. These attachments are also distractions from a life serving Spirit, Infinite Love; we cannot give our power to the ego, the deceiver, and still serve love. We cannot tell our spouses we forgive them and then continually hold them accountable to the past. We cannot fear losing all our earthly material belongings and still have faith and trust in a higher power who loves us and wants the best for us – these are all attempts to serve two realities, which is impossible. Each time I enter a moment of fear around lack or scarcity, I reflect on moments when divine intervention has shown up in my life.

I am often reminded and shared with friends to stress I have nothing to fear when I had $395.00 in my bank account on the day rent was due. The rent cheque for $1,200.00 had already been deducted from my bank account, which meant I had a balance of minus $805.00. I had until 5 pm, and the bank would close out their daily transactions to deposit the difference so my rent would not bounce. I prepared myself for that uncomfortable phone call to my landlord when the mail arrived at 3 pm. There was an unexpected cheque from my insurance company for $800.00 from a deductible taken the previous year, and they were returning it to me because it was deemed a not–at–fault accident. I fell to my knees in deep gratitude, reverence and awe of my heavenly Mother, who once again showed me her devout love for me; I was entirely in the hands and heart of her. Letting go of our attachments to our ego and false physical power is a constant, daily occurrence. We must continually ask ourselves, "Who am I serving in this situation, at this moment? I may not see Spirit in the traditional ways of the material world, but I have faith and trust in her infinite love, embracing and protecting me. I see Spirit with my heart and in her creations throughout the physical world. Every day, I am always provided with my daily bread.

Before the patriarchal churches we know of today, our ancestors celebrated our cyclical nature of birth–death–resurrection. Resurrection myths are not something new to Christianity; they have been around for thousands of years in almost every Goddess/God story. The death and resurrection myths were told to explain Earth's cycles. Hades took Persephone to the underworld, but she returns every spring to oversee the planting and ensure a good harvest for her people because of a deal made by her grieving mother, Demeter. The Goddess Isis scours the earth for her beloved Osiris' body parts and resurrects him through love to conceive their son Horus. Isis, Osiris and Horus's story was known as the Holy Trinity of Mother/Father/Child. It was told in Egypt for thousands of years, Isis is renowned for her resurrection myths and eternal life, and Osiris was the Egyptian God of resurrection. The main difference between these myths and the stories of Yeshua is that all the ancients started as Goddesses/Gods with tremendous powers.

Yeshua came as a man in a human body and was raised to a deity through his resurrection. We must remember that Romans edited the New Testament gospels to convert Roman pagans in a time of great political unrest. This was an attempt to unify all Romans in one universal belief system. The Romans always believed in Gods and Goddesses; therefore, Yeshua was presented as the only Son of God. In many apocryphal texts, Yeshua is named the Son of man, not the Son of God. Yeshua was a man who reached enlightenment and taught his disciples the path to understanding our true nature. I am the light, and the way has been interpreted for 2,000 years that Jesus is the only way to redemption. If this is true, why would he also teach that we do not need intermediaries to speak on our behalf with our Creator? He taught, "I AM is the light and the way." Our I AM Divine presence within us. When we know this, I AM presence and speak directly through prayer to our Divine Mother/Father; then we listen through meditation, the answers are revealed to us, our path is guided. Therefore, there is nothing to fear in the physical realm; absolutely nothing can harm our true nature. The Master of the world must deny us, for we have overcome his power over us.

This was the most challenging chapter for me to write. It paralyzed me for more than three weeks that I completely stopped writing. Following an inspirational conversation with my brother and closest spiritual friend Reverend Daniel Wright, I worked through my fears to process this very human side of myself. This writing was never meant to appear as though

I had reached Yeshua and Miryam's enlightenment level, and I felt like a hypocrite trying to process the message in this section. I now embrace that every day I participate and honour my divinity through prayer, meditation, gratitude journaling, cooking meals for my family with love and gratitude. Like so many of us, I struggle daily with personal vices and genuine human struggles. At this time, my vices include cigarettes, and I enjoy a glass or two of white wine. Just as Ereshkigel is Innana's shadow self, I often have to descend into the underworld to heal ancient, deep emotional traumas. I recognize that my humanity's full spectrum is a moment-to-moment opportunity to embrace love, to be aware when the ego wants to snare me in. We must work each day to be better than the day before and embrace our full humanity with all of its joys and grief, achievements and struggles. As we continually turn our attention to the great indwelling power for guidance, this is the greatest gift. Each moment is another chance to choose love over fear and constantly shift our focus to Spirit's advice and support. Christ consciousness is not solely for Christians; it is a state of being, a way of conscious thought to follow a path of love, experiencing our humanity and our divinity fully. There will be internal conflict along the course, and we will not always get it right. Once we surrender to Infinite Love, the suffering we experience physically will help us cultivate an inner strength that connects to the power that connects all creation.

> "The question is not will you face hardship or adversity. The question is how you will face it when it inevitably comes." Author unknown

Heart Chakra – Receive the energy of love, radiate this essence

The fourth chakra, also known as the heart chakra (Anahata), is located in the chest's center. This chakra is all about love. In its highest form, this love is all-embracing and Infinite. When we feel Infinite love, we do not judge others and live in harmony with all creation; we realize that we have nothing to fear from our heart space because we are not just our physical bodies; free of the flesh's weakness, the illusion of our fears. When our energy goes down through this chakra, it becomes a love based on restrictions. When this energy goes upward, we look at all of creation through the lens of love and are beginning to vibrate at a higher level, unconditional love and devotion. The heart is the mid-way point between the chakras attached to our physical existence and the upper chakras connected to Spirit; the heart is the bridge between the two. When we receive the energy of love, we have no option but to radiate this essence outward to the world, and the healing of creation begins in this simple action. The colour associated with this chakra is green with a vibrational frequency of 540-570 THz

My Soul Speaks

Live as your authentic self; the more you live connected to your soul, the better you can interpret the guidance you receive. Enjoy the moment, and then you start living your dreams – leaps get more manageable when you take baby steps (Inspired Action.) You are on a journey of reconnecting with your inner wisdom. When you are insecure or unsure about the future, keep putting one foot in front of the other, keep doing what is in front of you with all your heart and love and what is meant for you will always find you.

Affirmation

Today I release judgment of what I perceive as my shortcomings and replace it with compassion and love for my journey. If any person, place or thing annoys me, I will return my vision to see it through the lens of love. I will have the courage to try in each moment to overcome my fears of lack, scarcity or unworthiness and have faith that a divine plan is always working for the greatest good of humanity's evolution.

Exercise

Once again, make sure you have your pen and journal with you. Breathe deeply into your heart, imagine a glowing emerald green light filling your heart space, expanding in all directions. Ask yourself, "What currently has power or authority over me?"

- Write down three things in the physical world you cannot live without which offer you immediate personal gratification.
- Next, dig deep within and discover what you truly fear; what you are afraid of will happen if this person, place, thing, status-quo is taken from your life.
- Continue doing this while questioning two things; what has power over me, and what do I attempt to control out of fear?

Example:

Power   **Fear**

Job/loss of job   Security, failure, poverty

Prayer

Great Infinite Love, the creator of all, help me to see my fear of failure, security and poverty (replace with any fear that has come up for you) as illusions of my head-brain, of my temporal senses. Help me to see with my heart that everything happens as part of a Divine plan; I am perfect exactly the way I am. My false sense of security is a construct of my ego, fill me with the knowledge that all is well no matter what "appears" to be happening in my physical world. I ask that Divine Love heal my fears and guide me on my path for the greatest good of all.

Meditate

Close your eyes and take three deep breaths in through the nose and out through the mouth, feel yourself moving your attention within.

Imagine a golden cord attached to the base of your spine travelling through the earth, through soil and rock to the centre of Mother Gaia, see her radiant heart and connect your golden cord to her heart. Feel her infinite love travelling through the golden cord back up through the Earth and into your body, lighting each chakra with a brilliant golden light. Up through the root, travelling upwards through the sacral, solar plexus, heart, throat, third eye and out through the Crown up to the heavenly realms, connecting with our beloved divine Father. Bring the love and light back down your golden cord, through the crown, back down into the heart where the trinity unites, Mother, Father, Child. Feel the intense infinite love permeate your entire being; all fears dissolve into the no-thingness when the trinity is united.

When you are ready, wiggle your toes and stretch your fingers, feeling back into your body and open your eyes. Know love is your true nature, and the love of Infinite Source is with you at all times.

CHAPTER 12

FIFTH BOUGH – CLARITY AND TRUTH

Reject the Deceiver

"When you have rejected the deceiver, can you
pass through the hardest gate of all, to attain
the fifth bough and the fruit of clarity and truth
of your soul and, knowing yourself for the
first time as a child of the living Spirit."[66]

A S WE SAW AT THE FOURTH GATE, THE DECEIVER IS THE MASTER of the World, the physical world, our ego. It is only in rejecting the illusion that our ego or this material world is our home that we emerge into pure consciousness and become a vehicle to carry the message of love. We see with clarity and truth our true nature, a child of the living Spirit, Infinite love. When we relinquish power and surrender fully into trust and faith that Spirit has a Divine Plan, we can flow with life.

The Gospel of Thomas speaks of this. As you remember who you are, you are like an identical twin with all of creation. "If those who lead you say to you, look, the kingdom is in the sky; then the birds will get there first. If they say it's in the ocean, then the fish will get there first. But the kingdom of God is within you and outside of you. Once you come to know yourselves, you will become known. And you will

---

[66] Quillan, D. J. (2010). *The Gospel of the Beloved Companion: The Complete Gospel of Mary Magdalene.* CreateSpace Independent Publishing Platform. 42:10

know that it is you who are the children of the living Father."[67] The Gospel of Thomas saying 3. Yeshua has repeatedly taught that we are all children of the living spirit and that the kingdom is within each of us. "Neither shall they say, Lo here! or, lo there! for, behold, the kingdom of God is within you."[68] (Luke 17:21)

As Miryam's heart and mind are purified of judgement, wrath, ignorance, intolerance, duplicity, arrogance, weakness of the flesh and conquering the illusion of her fears, she is entering the peace of pure consciousness. This, the master tells her, is the greatest gift of all. When we have released all ties and false beliefs in our limited physical perceptions, our senses, we see with clarity and truth our authentic self always guided and connected to the One unity consciousness.

When Yeshua and Miryam began their ministry in the world, both had already mastered their energy; they spent years practicing these skills. They taught that you must first be at peace with your inner world to create the outer world you want. Meditation is a powerful tool for tuning into our inner guidance and can direct spiritual enlightenment. In this deep state of meditation, we can also receive information from the ethereal realms connected to our inner compass. When we enter into deep meditation, we detach from the world of form entangled in the duality of emotions, materialism, and the chatter in our minds. Our soul can travel past the physical plane into the Heavenly realms within, joining with the guidance of angels and ascended masters who are waiting for us to ask for their help. In many of the apocryphal texts, it is explained that Yeshua had the ability to bi-locate (be in two places at the same time.) Living from the light body with its freedom was available to all initiates willing to do the work described and fully realize their divinity. Yeshua's ability to bilocate was not physical; he had transcended the limits of time and space. Each of us does this in our

---

[67] Meyer, M. W., Pagels, E. H., Robinson, J. M., Funk, W., & Poirier, P. (2009). *The Nag Hammadi Scriptures: The Revised and Updated Translation of Sacred Gnostic Texts Complete in One Volume* (1ˢᵗ ed.). HarperOne. (The Gospel of Thoms Saying 3.)

[68] Haynes, C. L., Jr, Haynes, C. L., Jr, Baker, L. L., & Danzey, E. (n.d.). *The Bible - Read and Study Free Online*. Bible Study Tools. Retrieved January 5, 2021, from https://www.biblestudytools.com/Luke 17:21

dream state; our souls leave our bodies and reconnect with the ethereal realms of the Angels, Ascended Masters and ancestors; we are briefly reunited and encouraged by them. Being born into the dense matter of Earth is an honourable decision; the heavenly realms bow to us for accepting this monumental task of evolving humanity. Yeshua reminded us continually of this infinite power, our ability to connect with Infinite Love and separate ourselves from earthbound consciousness.

The work is not easy, and you will have to be consciously aware at all times of every thought and emotion as it arises. Yeshua spent forty days alone in the desert, in prayer and meditation, purifying himself for his enormous calling and receiving his guidance. Most of us cannot leave our lives for six weeks, but we can prioritize our spiritual practices. We recently had our niece stay with us, and she commented how nice it was that we all sat down to dinner every evening as a family, and even nicer, we do not leave the table after we have cleared the dishes. After dinner is our time to catch up, learn about each other's day and connect. Dinner together is non-negotiable in our house; if you are home, you are expected at the dinner table. My spiritual practice is the same; my daughter painted a sign for my bedroom door that says, "Fuck off, I am meditating, Namaste." Many may take offence to the swearing, but it is a play on words that informs everyone; my meditation time is sacred to me; if the sign is on the door, please respect my space. It is easy to binge-watch Netflix and zone out, but as said before, the only way up is in, and regular spiritual practice of prayer, meditation, journaling is the only way, and it does get easier with practice.

I am reminded of an old saying, "God will not give you more than you can handle." The birth of my first son was a complicated, three-day ordeal; my body was beaten and exhausted; I was twenty-four and had no idea how I would make it another moment. At this exact moment, the divine within me knew that for me to birth this new life, I would have to transcend my physical body and allow my Divine Mother to assist me. I recall the exact moment twenty-six years ago when I surrendered to her, and I cried out, I cannot do this on my own, I cannot go on. At that moment, I felt a strength overtake me I had not known I possessed, and I believe my son felt it as well. With an oxygen mask on my face, the support of my husband urging me on and the undeniable presence of the Divine, my son burst forth into this world, a colossal 9 pounds 12 ounces. The arduous journey through the birth canal, entering the world of the physical, was evident in my son's body. He was born with a black eye, bodily bruises, dents in his temples from the forceps, and a deep bruise on the top of his head from the vacuum. He was not breathing when he entered this world, the cord wrapped around his tiny neck, doctors and nurses were running into the room in a frenzy to the loudspeaker announcing code blue in obstetrics room four. I recall staring at my mother and sister's faces, their horror that my baby, after all of this, was not going to live registered, and I began screaming. The moment I heard him cry for the first time, my entire body shook with uncontrollable tears. It was only on his third day in this world when we were finally home from the hospital; I sat in the shower, the hot water pouring down on me, purifying my body and soul that I sobbed and I prayed, the enormity of what we had both been through finally releasing. I thanked the Great Mother for her intervention in assisting me with the birth, but most importantly for the beautiful child she had brought into my life, into my protection and care. I knew, in that instant, the unconditional, infinite love the Divine has for us, and I made a promise to share this divine love with this child of light I was honoured to mother. His physical body and soul I was to nourish and help grow to assist him in realizing with clarity his divinity.

At this bough, Miryam's soul is called into transcendence and surrender of her will to the will of Spirit. The silence is a surrender to the power of your soul, and you relinquish your attachments to the five senses of physical reality and tap into the incredible power of your inner guide. Every word you speak is aligned with your authentic self; there is no longer desire for empty words; if we cannot communicate love and honour, silence speaks louder. Our souls crave silence; the peace that comes from being wholly captivated by direct contact with our divine self is immeasurable. "Mary was speaking, and she said, "Words have no meaning apart from the Mother Spirit, therefore, to know her is meaningful. Words have meaning to the extent that they invoke knowledge of her, but she is known only in silence."[69] The "voice of

---

[69] Malachi, T. (2006). *St. Mary Magdalene: The Gnostic Tradition of the Holy Bride (Gnostic (4))* (First Edition). Llewellyn Publications. p.161

the world," our head-brain or inner chatter, dissolves in a moment of divine consciousness. In union with the divine, the soul cannot hear anything of the outside world; the powers of the ego no longer enslave us. When we meditate, we are in touch with our true nature, infinity consciousness, where answers to our more critical questions are available. Aligned to our higher truth, no longer attached to the physical world's daily affairs, we live in the present moment and are guided for the highest good of all. As the world's voice is silenced and we connect with our higher truth, we become an instrument of peace and healing for the world. We live in flow, embodied in our human form and allow our physical existence to co-create with Spirit to fulfill our purpose in this lifetime. Our words and actions are fully aligned with our highest truth and communicated authentically. This is why this is the greatest bough of all; here we reach the peace we have been waiting for, we are free. Once Miryam saw with clarity and truth her true nature, she was no longer a disciple; she had become a teacher, Yeshua's identical twin.

In the 14th Century, a Christian mystic named Marguerite Porete wrote a book called "The Mirror of Simple Souls." Marguerite was part of a beguine group of women who were not bound by any vows as the nuns were but dedicated their lives in service to humanity on behalf of God. The Church targeted these women because they could not control them, continuously interrogating them and burning at the stake in Marguerite's case. Her writings declare a direct connection with God without the need for church masses or clergy. Marguerite states that she had a deep relationship directly with the divine, and therefore no other authority had any control over her. In her book, she shares at length annihilation, the death of our wills, to be replaced by only the will of God. She describes seven stages of annihilation the soul must go through to achieve Oneness with the divine. The number seven is a powerful spiritual number representing many paths to the divine; many journeys to enlightenment are described as seven paths mentioned earlier, so prominent, it deserves further acknowledgement. The number seven is a seeker of truth number, representing inner wisdom. In the Torah, God created the world in seven days. There are seven holy spirit gifts representing perfection (physical and spiritual). There are seven colours of the rainbow, and as explored here, seven chakras with coordinating colours of the rainbow (the rainbow light body). The number is often connected with spiritual awakening and the development of wisdom. For the human soul to reach its full potential, it must be free of attachments to wealth, physical appearance, judgement, shame, anxiety.

The Mirror of Simple Souls was written in old French and proposed a dialogue among the imaginative figures of Love, Reason and Truth. The Church had transitioned their elite male education to Latin in another attempt at control. If the majority cannot read the Bible, they cannot interpret it, and the priests become impenetrable. With this use of Latin, the first rise in suspicion would have been the use of Old French. Porete claimed the only authority over her life was God's authority for her religious experiences. When a soul is in mystic union with God, it no longer seeks anything outside of itself and becomes one with God. This book was popular and threatened the Church's authority, and they wanted to silence an independent and outspoken woman who posed a threat to their male-dominated religious hierarchies. "The Mirror of Simple Souls" copies were burned in front of Marguerite, and the church fathers commanded her to stop circulating them. She refused and spent a year and a half in prison in complete silence, communing only with God. In 1310, Marguerite was tried by the Church, and when she refused to recant, giving authority only to God as her advisor, she was burned at the stake as a heretic.

I abhorred confession in the Roman Catholic tradition; every three or four weeks having to bear my sins to the priest and receive penance was abominable. It felt like a double punishment; most of my transgressions had already been punished by parents or teachers; it was a re-traumatization of all the ways I was an unholy, bad girl. Unfortunately, my devout Mother would not allow us to take communion if it had been too long since our last confession; this was even more humiliating. Sitting in the pew, as everyone ushered down the aisle to receive the body of Christ, was like standing naked in a classroom. The knowing looks of my peers and fellow parishioners turned my already red freckled face crimson with shame, I was not right with God, and everyone knew it. Communion was a badge of honour we Catholics wore, showing the world that we were the chosen ones, the followers of the righteous hero, we ate the body of Christ, and he in return would absolve all our sins, or that is what it felt like to me. When I finally left the Catholic community, it was because numbers had been falling drastically over the years, and our parish priest would yell and shame us for not being regular attendees. He had implemented a sign-in sheet for every young man or woman preparing for communion and confirmation to prove they were attending mass each Sunday. Attending mass was personal for me, not a should, but want, and the shaming was the final straw that broke my faith in the Church, which had already weakened over the years when my inquisitive mind about the teachings had gone unanswered. I have spent the past fifteen years studying all religions, philosophies and beliefs. My bookshelves are filled with a vast array of mystical and esoteric teachings. Still, it was the call of the divine feminine energy, who had been calling to me all my life, that eventually restored my faith in an all-encompassing and loving creator.

On a hot summer evening in 1997, my husband was at soccer, and my two-year-old son was in a deep sleep. I set up my altar with a statue of "Our lady of la Leche" (the nursing mother, Mary). I had fallen in love with her at a gift shop in St. Augustine, Florida; there was a graveyard there that broke my heart, dedicated to all the unborn children and ones who died at birth. I had a prayer card dedicated to her and a single white candle along with the statue. I entered a deep trance-like state, and the world was silenced. I saw my maternal great-grandmother, grandmother, and father-in-law, who had recently passed away in a vision. In a slightly confused state, which often happens to me in deep meditation, I could sense each of them smiling at me and ushering me forward with a sweep of their arms, each of their faces smiling like Cheshire cats, as though they had a secret. When I reached the end, there was a glorious vision of Mother Mary, in all her beauty, a new mother, holding the baby Yeshua to her breast. Her smile was magnificent, and a deep peace came over me; just as I sensed she was about to speak, my baby monitor shrieked at total volume, ripping me out of my meditation. Anyone who has experienced this type of deep trance like meditation knows it takes time to acclimatize to the physical world when abruptly disturbed in this manner. As I attempted to shake off the confusion, staring at the baby monitor with all its lights flashing frantically, alerting a mother her child needs her, I initially stared in disbelief. My child was a toddler, and this was not registering with me; the cries were a very new baby, possibly only weeks old. I finally moved into action, running to my son's room; he was sound asleep in his race car bed. The monitor was still screaming and flashing from my bedroom. I yelled downstairs to my brother and his wife, who was staying with us at the time to come quickly. As they reached the threshold of my bedroom door, the monitor went dead, stopped, silenced, no lights. They both had heard nothing and stared at me with concern, contemplating having me committed to the psych ward, I am sure. It was 11:30 pm, and as I was putting on my shoes, asking them to listen for Christopher and grabbing my car keys, my husband arrived home. When I explained, in a calm but confident voice, I would buy a pregnancy test, it was clear to me this was the message in this vision; all three stared at me, perplexed. The pregnancy test was positive and confirmed a few days later at the doctor's office; the confirmation was "barely pregnant," meaning so newly pregnant the HCG levels were faint.

Recall that I believe the soul enters the fetus at 22 days when the heart starts beating. My new baby's soul announced his arrival in my body through ancestors who had passed and the divine feminine Mother Mary. The identical ancestors and a divine feminine presence were with me through my labour and the birth of this child. I had chosen midwives for this birth; the previous hospital birth had left a trauma in my body. As I lay in the jacuzzi, approaching the final moments of active labour, I had no pain. I was in the room on my own as my husband and mother had stepped out to speak with the midwife. Upon their return, they later explained that I was in a trance-like state, entirely still, laying in the fetal position. They began to speak to me, and I put my finger to my lips and whispered, "Sssh, you will make them go away; they are massaging my body to ease the pain." I then continued like this for the next hour until it was time to bring him into the world. I do not remember very much of this; it was relayed to me in detail by my husband. He and my mother said they exchanged glances because the jacuzzi jets were not on; they had assumed this was what I was referring to and proceeded to move into the background, sitting silently not to disturb me.

Our ancestors work with Spirit and the angelic realms to come to our aid for everything; all we have to do is call to them. They will never interfere with our free will, but they are waiting for our call. Mirayam's message of direct divine connection and the ego's shedding to reach our full potential has miraculously continued to be taught in secret. This message has been kept alive through the centuries because it is truly the only path in the Way of the Heart and our transformation and evolution of humanity.

Throat Chakra – Aligned with the highest truth, communicate with love and honour, my words speak the truth of the universe and my authentic self

The fifth chakra (Vishudda) is in the throat area. In its highest form, we can express ourselves authentically, the truth of I AM. When we speak our truth, we live in peace, joy and confidence. When this energy goes downward through this chakra, we may feel uneasy and insecure. The fifth bough we recall was the most challenging gate to pass through, knowing your soul's clarity and truth and knowing you are a child of the divine. This is when we can speak with authenticity; live in the present moment, and easily experience divine energy. I work on clearing my throat chakra continuously; it seems to have a consistent block. I believe this is associated with more than this lifetime for me. The information I am sharing in this book is deeply personal, and for fear of persecution, a lot of the mystical experiences I have had have never been shared before. I trust now, this is the time I have been guided to share, and when my story is told, my throat will rejoice at me speaking my truth. The colour associated with this chakra is blue, with a vibrational frequency of 580–610 THz

My Soul Speaks

Expel the myth that is you. Let go of everything you have been taught thus far and let the new arrive. You may not trust it yet, but soon you will see the pieces come together one by one and fit within the grand design of life. Trust, let go, allow, be, but remember it is in unity where your strength lies. Alone we can do nothing; together, we can do everything. Our true nature is togetherness. Cultivate your connection to the Divine I AM presence. Ascend within, embody Divine Light. Become a conduit of a higher form of unconditional love and be an instrument of peace and healing in the physical world.

Affirmation

I see with clarity my oneness with the Earth and all creation. Therefore, I choose to be empowered by detaching from the limited physical realm and living the truth of my authentic self, a fully human and fully divine Being.

Exercise

Mantra Meditation

> The head-brains job is to create thoughts. The attempt to silence this brain often leads to frustration and blocks your ability to experience mindfulness. Mantras help us focus and stay in the present moment. Each time you feel thoughts arising, return to repeating a mantra silently and allow the thoughts to float by to be replaced with the mantra; this will continually bring you back to your practice.
>
> Get comfortable, preferably in a darkened room free from distraction. Close your eyes and focus on your breath, three deep inhalations through the nose and deep exhalation out the mouth, letting go of any tension or resistance.
>
> Set an Intention: May I enter the silence of Infinite love through my heart.
>
> Choose a mantra that resonates with you, aligned with what you want from your meditation.
>
> "I am divinely guided at this moment; I enter the silence of my heart."

Do this for as long as it feels necessary to release the incessant thoughts in your mind and draw you deeper into the silence. Then, each time your brain wanders, repeat your mantra.

When you are ready, release the mantra, return to your body, open your eyes, and return to the physical world.

CHAPTER 13

Sixth Bough – Power and Healing

> "When you truly have eaten of the fruit of
> clarity and truth of yourself, then could you
> partake of the fruit of power and healing.
> The power to heal your own soul."[70]

YESHUA AND MIRYAM LIVED AND TAUGHT A SIMPLE LIFE. YET, IT was so radically different, and the teachings became complicated. In contrast, God and the law were of utmost importance in mainstream church teachings. They introduced the Spirit, the feminine aspect of the Divine, the active principle that offers us true enlightenment. They brought us the teachings of wholeness, oneness in place of perfection. The word perfect keeps humanity in a cycle of shame and guilt, unable to reach a unified oneness with the Divine and fellow beings. In the attempt at perfection under the laws, we perpetually fail, every transgression punishable by our internal condemnation. Love and forgiveness were at the heart of the Nazarene teachings; each time we miss the mark is an opportunity to return to love, forgive ourselves, and connect with Spirit for guidance. According to Acts, "And the multitude of them that believed were of one heart and of one soul: neither said any *of them* that ought of the things which

---

[70] Quillan, D. J. (2010). *The Gospel of the Beloved Companion: The Complete Gospel of Mary Magdalene.* CreateSpace Independent Publishing Platform. 42:11 (page 118)

he possessed was his own; but they had all things in common."[71] (Acts 4:32–33) In uniting with Spirit, we see everything with one heart and one soul, equal; we belong to the Earth and possess nothing. When we cling to our illusion that we own anything, we create pain and suffering. True power lies in realizing our oneness with all of creation and Spirit.

Yeshua and Miryam were deeply rooted in the ancient wisdom teachings, where the soul's ascension was the primary goal of this human existence. The Essenes, with whom it is believed both Yeshua and Miryam were closely connected, felt in a perfect world; their primary goal was the human transformation of becoming a perfect human. I think this is where Yeshua brings his message, and the goal is not perfection, but once again, wholeness, the knowledge of oneness. Tibetan Buddhism greatly influenced the Essenes, and their beliefs and practices focused on achieving the celestial rainbow light body. Yeshua embodied these practices as a master and taught them to his disciples in many apocryphal gospels. Definitively in the Gospels of Mary and the Gospels of the Beloved Companion, Miryam reached this level of wholeness, as I believe so did Thomas and Phillip, all gospels deemed heretical and forbidden. A few devout Christians I know called the Gospel of Phillip "woo woo," describing Jesus as a flying outer spaceman." None of them had read any apocryphal gospels because the Bible teaches false prophets. In the Sermon on the Mount, Jesus warns of false prophets, [15] "Beware of false prophets, who come to you in sheep's clothing but inwardly are ravenous wolves. [16] You will know them by their fruits. Are grapes gathered from thorns, or figs from thistles? [17] So, every sound tree bears good fruit, but the bad tree bears evil fruit. [18] A sound tree cannot bear evil fruit, nor can a bad tree bear good fruit. [19] Every tree that does not bear good fruit is cut down and thrown into the fire. [20] Thus you will know them by their fruits."[72] (Matthew 7:15-20) Once again, we listen with our hearts and feel the truth of the words hidden within this sermon. The tree and the fruits are referred to continually in teachings for thousands of years in many traditions as

---

[71] Haynes, C. L., Jr, Haynes, C. L., Jr, Baker, L. L., & Danzey, E. (n.d.). *The Bible - Read and Study Free Online*. Bible Study Tools. Retrieved January 5, 2021, from https://www.biblestudytools.com/Acts 4:32-33

[72] Ibid:71. Matthew 7:15-20

the tree of life, which is also the critical element in the Gospel of the Beloved Companion. I believe the Roman editors may have twisted the narrative, instilling fear in this sermon of anyone who did not agree with the books they chose for the New Testament. Jesus informed his disciples to beware of the Pharisees and Sadducees, who believed they had the only authority of "Gods" strict laws. Later, the church fathers would lead humanity away from the knowledge of their internal divine connection, denying direct communication with Infinite Source. The original teaching, unedited in the apocryphal gospels, teaches the fruit as the elixir of life when consumed or better explained as living from higher virtues of love overcomes our guardians' egoic self. Let's read this sermon from the book of Matthew in this context. We are informed that Jesus is teaching, if your roots are firmly grounded in the truth of your connection with Spirit, you will not produce false attachments to the ego, and its guardians will have no power over you. The only authority in our lives is Spirit, who resides within our hearts; the false prophets are our ego desires; when we allow the ego to lead our lives, we will bear bad fruit, pain and suffering. A person who lives an enlightened way will still have painful experiences in this human existence, people we love will leave the Earth, friends may betray us, but we will not view the suffering from the ego and will know that our Creator is not punishing us for transgressions; these are lessons for the evolution of our soul. I do not propose to understand the fundamental nature of Infinite Source, nor why seemingly terrible things happen, and I am not trying to diminish anyone's grief or pain. Still, I know the peace of surrender and the love I feel when my heart connects with Spirit. The Way of the Heart taught in the Gospel of the Beloved Companion, which I have been practicing and following while writing about it, is a path to rediscovering our divine selves. I believe that as more of humanity awakens to these teachings, embracing the masculine and feminine aspects of Spirit within each of us, we will stop creating a world of pain and injustices.

Just as Buddhism teaches, all are capable of becoming buddhas, so Yeshua and Miryam taught we all have the potential to become Ihidaya, enlightened ones, at our core, we are all pure and luminous, children of the light. The world was living under Roman rule, ingrained in the material world with rigid social customs and dogma, with the constant threat of persecution and death. Yeshua and Miryam's work together was to bring humanity out of the densest time in our existence and closer to the Light of infinite love, Spirit. Every spiritual master who arrives on this earth realm to assist humanity in evolution must train rigorously for their soul to be purified and available for this extraordinary task. Siddhartha Guatama, the Buddha, travelled for six years seeking the meaning of life through his teachers, but it was when he went into the silence of his heart under the bodhi tree that he found his true nature. The impermanence of our thoughts and emotions transformed into the delightful realization that we are both a body and a soul is an empowering awakening. This realization for the initiate leads them to experience their existence with clarity and truth as an expanded awareness of the One. Personal interests are set aside, actions are demonstrated through the higher self, in attunement with the highest good of creation. Roman domination suffocated the people with a corrupt government and insufferable violence, halting the evolution process. Crucifixion was a daily occurrence in the days of Roman occupation; slaves and the followers of intuitive or gnostic Christianity faced gruesome death by crucifixion if tried and accused in the Roman courts. The early Christians were persecuted and murdered for hundreds of years for spreading what the church deemed heretical information that threatened the hierarchy of the church and government. Yeshua and Miryam came to spread the good news of a better way of living through infinite love from the heart. The ascension process of going within and performing miracles was suppressed by Roman rule and later by the Roman church. Yeshua and Miryam showed us a different possibility of living on this planet in peace and harmony. They taught us that miracles are our natural state and that we have the power to heal ourselves and each other. This is not about discarding the physical world but about detaching from its power and authority over the soul, a transcendence of physical reality's five sensory worlds, into a love affair with our intrinsic reality of being a conduit on the earth realm for the greatest good of all creation. Ultimate power comes when we realize our intimate relationship with the indestructible force within us, connected and guided by the power of the love of our

Infinite Creator, as Joan of Arc declared; "I am not afraid, I was born to do this."

It takes great inner power and fortitude to live this message and share it with others during such tumultuous times, when death was an inevitable outcome, showing us the state of consciousness of Yeshua and Miryam. The message they shared was radically different from the mainstream religion taught in their day in the western world. The idea that we all could access the divine and heal ourselves and our Earth eventually led Yeshua to the Roman courts; the Pharisees were afraid of his power. The Romans were threatened by the idea that their hierarchy would crumble. A key element of their teachings was the balance between a Mother/Father God as reflected throughout the universe. Once we realize the importance of balancing both the masculine and feminine energies within ourselves, we can heal. Feminine energy is described as intuitive, nurturing, collaborative, to name a few; when out of balance within, these energies portray outwardly as people-pleasing, critical, needy and over-giving. Masculine energy offers stability, support, and decisiveness; this energy shows up as controlling, aggressive, and confrontational when out of balance. Once again, we are all created in the image of Spirit, a healthy balance of both masculine and feminine energies within, portrayed outwardly as a kind and caring person who takes action and makes decisions. Balanced light energy emanating within and from our physical body is the image of the indestructible life force energy that pulses within us and throughout the known universe and beyond, connecting everything in a joyous dance of creation. Miryam would have been a significant threat to the patriarchal churches, an empowered woman, a Priestess, a realized human, fully embraced in the light. She was the spiritual partner and collaborator of Yeshua, an authority on the teachings of the way, and a leader of the disciples. Before Yeshua guided her in the ascension teachings, she had already become a master of the ancient teachings of the mystery schools. In combining their divine energy to heal those who followed and all of humanity, they were uplifting the Earth's consciousness; this balance of energies is what is required now, in our turbulent times. Unfortunately, the patriarchy was too thoroughly ingrained in the logical mind, the outer world and their material attachments. A female leader who taught radical news of seeing with the heart and oneness with the divine had to be silenced by minimizing her role in Christianity. The discovery of the apocryphal texts is an opportunity for today's churches to re-evaluate the enormous importance of Yeshua and Miryam's dedication and devotion to the evolution of human consciousness. In Barbara Thiering's book Jesus and the Riddle of the Dead Sea Scrolls, she explains that the name Miriam in Hebrew and later Mary or Maria in Greek, Mery in Egyptian, was a title given to Essene women who were prophetesses and brides of the David kings. Mary goddesses carried sacred wisdom from ancient teachings.[73]

2,000 years appears to be a very long time for this awareness to grow and evolve, but time is an illusion of this physical reality; it does not exist outside this realm. As we enter a new age, we have been experiencing a global mass movement worldwide searching for the divine feminine. The divine energies of these beautiful souls are reawakening globally, and we are no longer afraid of speaking from our authentic truth. Priestess and mystery schools are re-emerging, and we are beginning to question the stories that have been taught for millennia, the tales which kept us oppressed. In 2001, I was offered the opportunity to buy a yoga studio. I had been practicing yoga regularly since 1987 and, for twelve years, had to drive over an hour twice a week to participate in a class with an advanced yogi. As my family grew, it became more challenging to continue the distance; I found a small studio in my town that offered myself and some friends private classes around our hectic schedules. Two years later, the instructor wanted to move and approached me as an avid student and asked me if I could purchase her studio. At that time, it would have been a bad investment of our finances and would likely have led me to bankruptcy, and I was happy being a student. It would have cost every cent of our savings and did not seem like a viable investment; the yoga wave had not yet started to trend in the West. Eleven years later, yoga studios began popping up everywhere, everyone had caught on to the benefits, and it became cool to say you practiced yoga. My teacher Axel, where I attended for twelve years, was an illuminated

[73] Thiering, B. (1992). *Jesus & the Riddle of the Dead Sea Scrolls: Unlocking the Secrets of His Life Story* (1st HarperCollins ed). HarperCollins.

yogi practitioner, not just an instructor. Students could not advance beyond the beginners' yoga unless they fully embraced the lifestyle, no meat, abstinence from alcohol, and other restraints conducive to the Niyama of self-discipline, which would fall in line with the ego guardian weakness of the flesh. Yoga practice is traced as far back as 5,000 years; their Yamas and Niyamas are an ethical code, similar to the way of the heart, the path taught by Miryam. It took 5,000 years to see more people embrace yoga in the Western world, and it has improved the lives of those who practice consistently. 2,000 years after so many early Christian stories were never told, burned or buried deep in the belly of Mother Gaia, they are finally resurfacing and openly being circulated to the masses. These findings help us to understand the true mission of the early disciples, the importance of the feminine in their ministry, and, most importantly, the state of consciousness Miryam reaches in her committed, consistent spiritual practices.

Our family's dear friend started studying Reiki and energy healing in the 1980s. Friends and family called her a quack, and it took her many years to grow her practice and "convince" people that we are energy and balance within our chakras and beyond could heal all sorts of ailments. It was the time of a great boom in the pharmaceutical industry, and the push for pills to ease our pain and illness instantly was at an all-time high. Reiki and energy work was the exact healing that Yeshua and Miryam performed 2,000 years ago. The church fathers explained Jesus' healing as a miracle only a Son of God could perform. They discounted the enormity of realizing that we have God-Energy that we can tune into to heal ourselves and others. Yeshua and Miryam laid the groundwork for what we see happening in our world today. In this new age of enlightenment, more and more people turn to natural medicine and energy healing for treatment from headaches to cancer. Our mind's power in healing first our soul and then physical or mental ailments within the body is a massive industry today.

In the canonical gospels and many apocryphal texts, Yeshua instructs his disciples to be as little children to enter the kingdom. "And said, verily I say unto you, except you be converted and become as little children, ye shall not enter into the kingdom of heaven."[74] (Matthew 18:3) As we have witnessed, the kingdom in Christianity became a place "up there," a place we go after living a good and moral life on Earth. An attempt by the church fathers to create rules that would keep them in power and create the illusion of a civilized society. If we all believe that if we follow the bishops, priests, and government rules and be good boys and girls, have a miserable existence on earth and be content with it, we will be rewarded when we die. The kingdom is already here, within us and among us, a state of peace and joy we all have the ability to achieve NOW! To ascend into a fully divine being, we must first descend and face our darkness, our shadow selves and find a way to love and embrace these parts of ourselves. Miryam was facing her shadows at the first four boughs, feeling into them and choosing the higher path of Spirit. We must meet these facets of ourselves, release our attachment to the ego-self and bring love to our dark emotions in complete acceptance. As she describes her ascent to bough six, emptied of the illusions of duality, innocent as little children, open and accessible to the message from our higher self, we are then ready to accept the kingdom as our truth and be healed and whole. We must fully surrender, embrace our shadows and come to a place of complete innocence to transform into our highest self-realization. When we have gone to the darkest parts of our character, loved and accepted with compassion, we are ready to own every part of ourselves as human and divine; our power lies here, and this is what leads to healing. By being the light and living in mystic consciousness, we allow those around us to choose the path of ascension and conscious awareness. As we begin living a life of giving and receiving Infinite love, we show others the peace and tranquillity that comes from just being.

Yeshua was not a Messiah who came to save the Jews from Roman rule, nor was he a saviour. He was a man who accepted his guidance from the divine and followed his calling as a mystic and wisdom teacher. Both he and Miryam fully engaged in a consistent spiritual practice of expanding their awareness; they followed the path that was asked of

---

[74] Haynes, C. L., Jr, Haynes, C. L., Jr, Baker, L. L., & Danzey, E. (n.d.). *The Bible - Read and Study Free Online*. Bible Study Tools. Retrieved January 5, 2021, from https://www.biblestudytools.com/Matthew 18:3

them, transforming human consciousness. They did not ask why or what the outcome was; they accepted their calling to serve humanity. We spoke in earlier chapters about following our souls' calling, so many of us are afraid to do this because we doubt the small voice that speaks to us. What if, like Yeshua and Miryam, we are asked to leave everything we know behind? What if we are asked to walk the earth and share the good news? What if we are asked to build an ark? The good news is, everything asked of us will be supported; when we move in the direction of the voice within, support from every realm will show up; we are never alone.

The gospel of Phillip 83,30-84,14 says: "The word says, if you know the truth, the truth will set you free."[75] (also John 8:32). Ignorance is a slave; knowledge (gnosis) is freedom. We have been ignorant of the truth for long enough. We must instill knowledge now, learn to trust the voice within as our life force energy and authority, our lives will find joy and fulfillment. We can continue to play out the old stories of injustice and disconnection or birth a new level of interconnectedness with the divine and all creation. We have the power to heal the hurt parts of ourselves and Mother Earth when we see with clarity and truth our true essence.

---

[75] Meyer, M. W., Pagels, E. H., Robinson, J. M., Funk, W., & Poirier, P. (2009). *The Nag Hammadi Scriptures: The Revised and Updated Translation of Sacred Gnostic Texts Complete in One Volume* (1st ed.). HarperOne. (The Gospels of Phillip 83,30-84,14).

Third Eye Chakra – Open mind, expanded awareness, and experience through Higher Self

The third eye (Ajna) chakra is located between the brows (positive pole), where our spiritual eye resides, knowing a connection with the Divine. Situated at the skull base (negative pole) in the medulla oblongata, this is where our ego lives. The power to heal your soul is possible when our state of consciousness moves this energy upwards in this chakra, connecting us to our higher soul.

The sixth chakra's positive pole is between your eyebrows and is referred to as the "third eye" or "spiritual eye." When energy is blocked in this chakra, you become set in your ways, relying only on factual, scientific evidence and ignoring your intuition's wisdom. When open, you have a balance of your analytical mind and your intuition. Now is when you have the power to heal your soul; you are the master of oneself, non-material with total vision. Many lightworkers believe the dark forces have made several attempts to keep humanity's third eye closed, so we remain in the dark about our true essence. The use of fluoride in our drinking water and toothpaste is one way the pineal gland becomes calcified. Descartes called the pineal gland the seat of the soul. The colour associated with this chakra is indigo with a vibrational frequency of 610–670 THz

My Soul Speaks

I have the power to heal my soul and therefore be free of dis-ease. Follow your heart. When you go out into the world, be light of nature and be joyous and grateful in life. Be present at the moment and fill yourself with the light of each moment, of each person you encounter. Listen deeply into your heart, not to words. Yeshua taught us that those with the ears to hear should listen, not with our physical ears, with the inner hearing.

Affirmation

I trust my inner guidance to give me the power to heal my mind, body and soul. I surrender my ego to this guidance and know my highest realization is leading me.

Exercise

Consciously examine why you do things, are they selfish, separation consciousness, or are they focused on the highest good for all? Universal?

Stay aware throughout each choice you make, ask yourself, why am I doing what I am doing? Is this fueling my ego desires which are fleeting and never fulfilled, or will it serve the universe?

Keep a notebook of each choice and examine it at the end of each day. Once you gain greater clarity of why you are doing something, you can consciously choose universal wellness.

Example: If I eat a Big Mac, large fries, and a coke for dinner a couple of days a week, I fuel my own personal desire. I know that this way of eating will eventually lead to obesity, clogged arteries, heart attack and the likelihood of early physical death.

If I choose to eat healthy to keep my physical vessel in optimum shape to carry out my Spirit-mission during this embodiment, I choose for the greatest good of all.

We can examine every choice, small or large and determine our motives and choose differently!

CHAPTER 14

SEVENTH BOUGH – FILLED WITH THE LIGHT AND GOODNESS

Free from all Darkness

"And I saw my soul, now free of all darkness, ascend
again to be filled with the light and goodness that
is the Spirit. And I was filled with a fierce joy as
my soul turned to fire and flew upwards."[76]

LIGHT AND GOODNESS ARE POWERFUL SPIRITUAL ENERGIES THAT permeate our beings allowing us to access the highest level of consciousness, a multidimensional, harmonious dance of consciousness. Miryam has released ego and karmic attachments and activated the chakra energy centres by removing lower desires and replacing them with positive emotions. In the arts of alchemical transformation, she has activated the light body, with the ability to heal and transform all who come in contact with her, consciously united with Spirit. In this dimension, we have healed our wounds and freed our souls. Darkness, pain, and suffering still exist in the outer world, but we have cultivated an inner strength to bring light to the shadows even if the worst imaginable happens. Our souls are pure light, pure love, at One-ness with Spirit. This transcendence of consciousness is the

---

[76] Quillan, D. J. (2010). *The Gospel of the Beloved Companion: The Complete Gospel of Mary Magdalene.* CreateSpace Independent Publishing Platform. 42:12 (page 119)

sole purpose of our lives. As we evolve, we break through the limiting beliefs of our tiny world and realize the great Oneness of the Universe. Once we reach this level, the fierce joy allows us to continue living in this chaotic world while remaining entirely at peace. Love becomes our guide; we release all duality and live in Oneness of the Universal Cosmic Heart.

When any initiate in the biblical stories encounters the Divine, there is the description of fire and flames. Fire is purifying, represents a cleansing of the old for new life and renewal, perfect holiness. In this part of the vision, Miryam sees her "soul turn to fire." Miryam has reflected on the character of her soul in the light of the Divines' blazing glory, which is all-consuming. The Goddess Isis is a fiery goddess called the Lady of Light and Flames in a papyrus from Oxyrhynchus. The fiery Isis represents healing and initiation. In the ancient myths and mystery schools, Isis initiates with fire to purify the ego (the mortal self) to bring us closer to the Divine. Isis's grandfather was the Sun God Ra, the living fire. The light is the silence when our soul has become wholly united with Spirit.

The way to achieve this is to let go of our past, surrender to any future outcome and live only in the present moment. As we let go of grievances, judgements or notions about any person, place or thing and live only in the here and now, our reward is the grace of Infinite Love. Give all past hurts over to the flames and watch them burn away. Surrender to whatever is presented to you at any given moment, knowing the eternal self is never separate from the infinite love and glory of Spirit. If we judge things as good or bad, we hold ourselves in limited, constrained energy, unable to accept each moment as a gift for our soul's evolution and humanity. In our current culture, we often want to fight something that we feel is hurting people, Fight to Conquer Cancer; both the words fight and conquer keep us in a violent state and work opposite to what we want to achieve. Mother Teresa so eloquently said, "Let us more and more insist on raising funds of love, of kindness, of understanding, of peace. Money will come if we seek first the Kingdom of God – the rest will be given."

Perhaps Love and Kindness to release cancer from our energy would be more appropriate. If the entire Universe held global meditations where all of humanity's attention was on relieving the human race of disease, we would eradicate these afflictions. Mother Teresa always said that she would attend a peace rally, but not a fight for something. Our world is in a chaotic state of violence, upheaval and darkness; it is time to put this behind us. Release our war-torn histories, leave night behind us, and be filled with so much joy and peace. The current political and socio-economic upheaval globally, but especially prevalent in the United States of America, is focused on what is happening and the past. Black Lives Matter is about the current injustices and the injustice of hundreds of years of slavery and brutality. We are culminating in a breaking point where another civil war is plausible. Slavery in the United States in its enormity was a very dark time in human history. We are currently witnessing that neither black nor white Americans have ever forgotten it. Deep hurt and shame still live in our consciousness because they have been passed down from generation to generation.

I had several friends of Irish Catholic descent in high school born in Canada; they were Canadian. One Summer, one of these friends went to Ireland and returned to tell us with pride that she had gone out with her cousins and kneecapped a protestant (kneecapping is a form of malicious wounding). I was speechless and felt ill. Her family moved to Canada to leave the violence behind and create a better life in our country. Still, they continued to share their stories and hatred about the protestant domination in Ireland with their children, which kept the hate alive. When these friends found out my father was protestant, they questioned how I attended a Catholic high school. They were horrified that my Catholic mother married the enemy; most of these friendships dissolved over a short period. Now is time to release the past to the flames, stop insisting on sharing the negative energy with future generations, we can all move into the light and goodness. Children are not born racist; this is taught to them by their adults. Begin teaching the children about unity and the illusion of separation. Teach them love, at the deepest level for all of humanity and our world's creations.

My discomfort with church and religion is that I witness hatred against fellow humans and earth creatures by church-going Christians. I cannot comprehend leaving a church service to spew hate on our fellow beings or toss garbage out the window of our car and pollute our earth.

We need to take a rugged look at the religions of today. Many churches create separateness; they create a superiority/inferiority complex and are often exclusive. We must learn that the truth lies within our hearts and search for it there. We have been accustomed to looking to the outside for authority in our lives. Now is the time to look within, follow the path taught 2,000 years ago of kenosis, completely emptying ourselves and surrendering our own will to follow the guidance of Spirit in all things.

It is time to relinquish the darkness from our beings by releasing all of this judgement, hatred, fear, anger to the flames and reach for the light. If we work together in cooperation and collaboration, and oneness instead of separation, we will fill our souls with more light and goodness, and there will be nothing but beauty and grace. Technology has propelled us faster than any other time in our history to collaborate with people all over the globe. Mass guided meditations with thousands of people online are commonplace. I have participated in several of these, from a Mary Magdalene heals the waters broadcast in France to a send love and rain to the forest fires of Australia, California and British Columbia, each separately. Thousands of people worldwide meditate together to heal Mother Earth; it is mighty. We are moving in the right direction; as the chaos rises, we reciprocate with worldwide love and peace.

Yeshua and Miryam are Master souls who incarnated as humans along with many others at a time of great strife and darkness in humanity. They came to bring the Light to the world and help us remember our light. We are light beings who radiate energy and consciousness. The darkness has made us so dense that very few of us can expand our awareness beyond this physical world. However, we are beginning to collaborate globally and see new ways of being, new possibilities, new vibrations of heightened consciousness and new perspectives of truth. We can raise our vibrations to the frequencies of light. We must release our fears, doubts and hatred to the fire which the light creates, to the flames of transformation. When we do this, we let in more light and become purer beings, vibrating our energy with more love and light. "Mary said, the spark must become a flame, and the flame must become a blazing fire. When you shine like the Sun, you will be complete."[77] The Divine Spark within us must be turned directly to Spirit in all things, being a beacon of light to humanity, in service to the good. Once the flame is lit, we have no choice but to become the Sun; it is our birthright.

Spiritual masters have described their meeting with the Divine and their I AM presence as fire, burning, flames. The fire of spiritual transformation is referred to as the violet flame or sacred flame. This flame is the ascension's balancing tool for karmic cleansing and to balance the divine masculine and feminine energies. All colours have a frequency; violet has the highest vibration of all colours; it carries love, forgiveness, spiritual transformation. Spiritual alchemists used fire's transformative healing properties for purification and transformed negative energy to a higher level of consciousness for all of creation. Miryam has raised her frequency to her crystalline solar light in this bough, embracing universal love and her I AM presence connected to Divine Source energy.

In St. Mary Magdalene, Malachi captures Mary's teachings from The Gospel of the Sophia Ain Sof (One-without-end), "God the Father entered in through the image of the Son, but the world was overwhelmed by the great supernal glory. Therefore, the Son imparted to the Mother Spirit and God the Mother has entered in through the image of the Daughter to nurture the little ones until they grow wise. The light entered, but was too bright, and so now the fire comes to purify so that all might be sanctified to receive the True Light. Everything shall be accomplished in due season, and it is the Mother Spirit that will accomplish everything."[78] (Malachi, 2006) The fires of transformation purify our souls in order that we may see the light of Mother Spirit; it is through recognizing and receiving her back into the world and in our hearts that we may heal, she will accomplish everything.

I belong to a wonderful networking group over Zoom; business owners, coaches, authors, and marketing experts worldwide. We meet once per week, morning for us here in Canada. Although the

---

[77] Malachi, T. (2006). *St. Mary Magdalene: The Gnostic Tradition of the Holy Bride (Gnostic (4))* (First Edition). Llewellyn Publications. P.158
[78] Ibid:77. page 146-47

discussions often share technology best practices for our business, they often veer towards a more spiritual nature. Dave Rogers of continual shift is a brilliant coach who has travelled the globe, studied under many masters and is a devoted divine masculine who honours the feminine, the goddess and the moon cycles. Dave leads our small group, and I mentioned how difficult it is for me to speak my authentic truth; I can write about it and then stumble, constantly clearing my throat chakra. At one of our meetings, when I had been invoking the violet flame for a few days prior, Dave said, "You have so much support here with our group to open your throat chakra; Bill is wearing blue, Dolly, Irene are wearing blue, and you are wearing violet." I was speechless; I was wearing all black. When the meeting ended, I immediately called my friend Bill and told him this experience; I believed Dave saw my light body, my aura, illuminated with the colour violet. I sent him a quick message describing this, and he responded with, "Brilliant and thank you for sharing, freakishly strange, wonderful, mysterious and so many miracles unfolding as we notice, invite, honour and invoke Miryam consciousness."

I invite you to watch some inspirational videos of Dave on YouTube. Continual Shift with Dave Rogers - YouTube.

Crown Chakra – Connection to Divine Source, Trust that I am the Light

The seventh chakra is at the top of the head, also known as the crown (Sahasrara) chakra. The colour associated with this chakra is violet, with a vibrational frequency of 670-750 THz. The crown is our connection to cosmic consciousness, united, where we join with Divine Energy in creative dance, with joy, peace and deep harmony. We are free from the darkness of the world and connected with the Source of all creation; here is where we meet our divine self, and the flames in our heart flare in deep reverence for our Creator and our true self. We are the alchemist, have no fear of death, Spirit flows through us, and every step we take is guided. Yeshua mentions the crown twice during the inner vision; once we have moved through our chakras and raised our frequency to higher vibrational emotions, there are no longer leaves (ego attachments) blocking the light of our essence.

My Soul Speaks

I had seen the Great Mother in the fullness of my heart when each baby was born from my womb, a gift from her vast womb. I had felt her presence when I needed courage and strength to keep going, exhausted with three children under the age of four. She held me with her gentle love, through joy and heartache, bliss and grief. The more I practice going inward to the silence in my heart, I find her light and see my beauty. I see the sacredness in everything through her eyes. Even a brief glimpse of her glory makes me ache for more. Light and goodness are not outside of us, not in relationships, lovers, family or friends; it always has been inside us. It is a love that is so intense and all-encompassing, eternal, and nothing we do will ever change this. So let Spirits fire burn within you, purify and cleanse the darkness, so you are filled only with light.

Affirmation

I am a divine being of light. Always connected to life force energy and Infinite love guides my every step.

Exercise

Violet Flame Meditation

There are no coincidences; an invisible force of Angels, Ascended Masters, and the unnameable love of Infinite Source always leads us. I felt stuck with my writing and so entered a quiet meditation asking for assistance. I will often turn to one of my oracle decks for guidance; this particular day led me to My Akashic Tarot deck by Sharon Anne Klinger and Sandra Anne Taylor. The card I choose from any deck never surprises me, but this one rendered me a sobbing mess for some time. The fourteenth card in the deck was "Initiation & The Count St. Germaine." It reads, "This card represents your initiation. It is much more than a change or even a transformation; it's nothing less than your movement into higher revelations of power, insight, and achievement. And the time is now."[79] It further informs us that we have been working with Ascended Masters for thousands of years toward a particular goal and service to humankind. At that moment, I knew beyond a shadow of a doubt; I was not writing a book; I was being guided by forces of love who were here to support the message of humanity's evolution and the path the Masters Yeshua and Miryam left for us to achieve a new state of being. Upon further research into the life of Saint Germain, there appeared little information. Once again, I was divinely guided to a book called "Violet Flame, to heal body, mind and soul" by Elizabeth Clare Prophet. Elizabeth and her husband, Mark, created the Summit Lighthouse, which focuses on raising humanity's consciousness. It is said that just as Jesus was the masculine avatar to bring enlightenment

---

[79] Klingler, S. A., & Taylor, S. A. (2017). *The Akashic Tarot: A 62-card Deck and Guidebook* (Tcr Crds/P ed.). Hay House Inc.

in the age of Pisces, Sainte Germaine will represent the masculine energy to bring in an enlightened age of Aquarius.

Finding a quiet space, if possible, outside under the Sun will help increase connection with this meditation; it is best to sit with your feet on the ground, arms and legs uncrossed.

Close your eyes and focus on your heart, relaxing deeper with each breath.

Ask the archangels and ascended masters for protection. "Archangels, Ascended Masters, please protect my crystalline light body from anything that is not for my or humanity's greatest good as dictated by Divine will."

Say your specific prayer for your healing and karmic cleansing, set your intention.

"Sacred violet flame, with my I AM presence, for the highest good of all, and only according to divine will, heal my heart and fill it with love, forgiveness and compassion. Transform negative energy from this life and all past lives into unconditional love and unity consciousness."

Invoke the violet flame from the affirmations given to us by St. Germain

I AM a being of violet fire,

I AM the purity God desires.[80]

Visualize a beautiful golden light filling the centre of your chest, your heart area; golden light is Christ's light.

---

[80] Prophet, E. C. (1958). *Summit Lighthouse*. Https://Www.Summitlighthouse. Org. https://www.summitlighthouse.org/violet-flame/

Feel this golden light course through your entire body, nourishing each chakra with light energy.

See the spark of a violet flame being lit in your heart centre and spreading beyond your physical body, surrounding the space and within you in vibrant violet light, the love extending beyond your feet and out through your crown chakra.

Repeat these decrees:

I AM a being of divine light

I AM a servant of Infinite light

I heal myself with violet fire to serve humanity

I AM a vehicle of higher consciousness bringing light to the world

Choose an area in your life you want to transmute from negative energy to energies of love, peace and forgiveness. Visualize this being burned by the violet flame and replaced with positive energy.

You can also send this positive energy out into the world, family and friends, or assist in societal issues. By visualizing the person or situation and sending love and forgiveness, you begin to heal for the greatest good.

When you are ready to close your meditation, bring the sphere of light and violet flame back into your body and imagine it settling in your third eye chakra.

Thank the Archangels and Ascended Masters for their protection and the violet flame for transforming negative energies. Thank you, thank you, Thank you.

CHAPTER 15

THE LIGHT BODY

GBC 42:13 "I beheld a woman of extraordinary beauty, clothed in garments of brilliant white. The figure extended its arms, and I felt my soul drawn into its embrace, and in that moment, I was freed from the world, and I realized that the fetter of forgetfulness was temporary. From now on, I shall rest through the course of the time of the age in silence."[81]

MIRYAM IS ENCOUNTERING HER PURE LIGHT ENERGY, HER crystalline body, and freed from the dense physical body and the attachments to the ego world; they no longer bind her, as she lives in a spiritual state of being. We are all capable of this ascension from the third-dimension reality, the physical world and egoic separation consciousness, to the fifth dimension, a higher state of unity consciousness. Miryam discovers herself in Divine Light, the Mother of all who birthed us from her dark womb into creation. She has followed the way to full empowerment and spiritual mastery by connecting with the Source of all within her. In raising her vibrational frequency from "I," the ego-self, to "We" unity consciousness, Miryam transforms, envisioning the world spiritually in place of materially. In the Sermon on the Mount, Jesus informs us that the only way to see God is to be pure of heart; we recall the original meaning of Virgin, *"Blessed are the*

[81] Quillan, D. J. (2010). *The Gospel of the Beloved Companion: The Complete Gospel of Mary Magdalene.* CreateSpace Independent Publishing Platform. 42:13 (page 119)

pure in heart, for they will see God,"[82] says (Matthew 5:8). Our true nature is that of high vibrational spiritual beings, living a virtuous life and replacing the lower negative thoughts discussed in the previous chapters with high vibrational virtues of love and compassion, peace and joy, makes us pure of heart, available to experience Spirit directly.

The Mystery school traditions and the Essene communities who influenced Yeshua's life and supported him in his great mission taught that the light body activated is merging our soul to spirit. Everything in the universe is a culmination of constantly moving energy creating matter. Quantum physics scientifically proves that 90% of our physical bodies are space and only 10% actual physical matter. Knowing how to harness the energy, using the physical body at its optimal level, with all energy centres (chakras) balanced, was Yeshua's primary teachings to humanity. Becoming a perfect light being, living in this ideal state of being, luminous and holy, was also the goal of the Essenes. Our energy field comprises many layers; the etheric body, emotional body, astral body and mental body are often used to describe our energy field. These are the denser forms of our energy.

The Merkaba is an Egyptian word translated as Mer (light), Ka (soul) and ba (body). We represent pure divine energy in the shape of two tetrahedrons that meet in the middle and form a three–dimensional energy field around the physical body. The Merkaba is activated through specific breathwork and meditation. It combines opposing energies of masculine and feminine in perfect harmony. Once activated, this harmony ignites your light body and assists in achieving higher consciousness. Some of the texts found at Qumran indicate that some communities were involved in Merkaba studies. For a more detailed analysis of the Merkaba, I suggest reading Drunvalo Melchizedek, The Ancient Secret of the Flower of Life. He is an expert in these studies and gives a thorough and practical application to activate them. The Universe is the manifestation of Source energy and extends beyond this, Eternal. Our denser physical forms are ready to transform living in the light, receiving the Grace from Spirit in pure unconditional love. Once

---

[82] Haynes, C. L., Jr, Haynes, C. L., Jr, Baker, L. L., & Danzey, E. (n.d.). *The Bible - Read and Study Free Online.* Bible Study Tools. Retrieved January 5, 2021, from https://www.biblestudytools.com/Matthew 5:8

the fire in our heart is lit, we realize our limitless being, the worldly things become meaningless and empty, and we become Oneness with the light. Yeshua said, "I AM the light and the way." His teaching is a radical movement from God outside to an individual ascension within our hearts, into purity out of the darkness of ignorance. His teachings were the Way of the heart. We are the light, cloaked in the robe of humanity!

Zoroastrians believed in the duality of Light – the good and Darkness – the evil, and they greatly influenced the Essenes. The Gospels of Mary (the authenticated versions) refer to Source as the good, the light. The Essenes were also greatly influenced by Egypt and the Pythagorean brotherhood, who taught that the soul could ascend to unite with the divine while embodied in the physical realm. Many of the disciples of Yeshua were too ingrained in their Judaic belief system and could not comprehend this radical gnostic movement of God in our hearts. From some of the recovered papyrus, we can see that Mary Magdalene, Thomas, Phillip and Mother Mary were among the few who truly understood their teacher's message. The church teaches that Jesus was resurrected in bodily form following the crucifixion; this has always made me imagine a zombie apocalypse. A master soul who taught his disciples not to worry about their bodies; it is temporary; it is difficult to comprehend that his final lesson for humanity would be to resurrect the body. "Mary said:" Many seek the resurrection of the flesh, but the superior resurrection is of the Spirit and is eternal. Seek always that which is superior." [83] We see in this paragraph; the lesson is the ascension of the immortal light body, or in Miryam and Yeshua's case, the rainbow body, living consciously connected to the divine within us and spirit in a frequency of unconditional love. The rainbow body is activated by living in the frequency of infinite love after the light body has been activated. Once we have released all judgment, we fully surrender our shadows and purify every thought; the rainbow body will activate. In living in this frequency of unconditional love, becoming the Completion of Completions, we achieve the rainbow body's ascension, which is superior to the flesh. Yeshua and Buddha

---

[83] Malachi, T. (2006). *St. Mary Magdalene: The Gnostic Tradition of the Holy Bride (Gnostic (4))* (First Edition). Llewellyn Publications. P. 163

both ascended and taught this path to their disciples. In their rendition of the resurrection, the Church has made it an almost impossible feat for feeble humans of original sin to attain enlightenment. They created Jesus as a Saviour-hero; now we can see him in truth; a spiritual master who came to earth to show us the way to the heart, entirely achievable for every human to ascend and live an enlightened and empowered life in physical form guided by Spirit, the good, creator of all.

When we manifested in this dense physical form following humanity's fall, we forgot our Divine nature. Miryam gives us hope in stating that forgetting is temporary; we are here to recall. It is difficult for many of us to remember when humanity lived in the higher dimension of our light bodies because we have been incarnating in this dense world for so long. Miryam reminds us that this world in physical form is an opportunity to awaken, to remember our multi-dimensional light beings of unconditional love. In the Secret book of John from the Nag Hammadi Scriptures, Yaldaboath Defiles Eve "The human beings were made to drink from the waters of forgetfulness."[84] Now is the time for humanity to remember; raise our consciousness to new enlightened levels of pure love and follow the Way taught by Miryam in its original teachings, or we will destroy our planet. Be freed from the attachments of the physical world and know that we are children of Divine light.

In this entire lesson, the most exhilarating line is that Miryam, with her inner vision, encountered an extraordinary woman, not a Father God. God the Mother is the one who met her within and embraced her. I have had inner visions where I have felt both a feminine and masculine energy, but to read this and know that the living spirit, clothed in the brilliant white of purity and holiness, is feminine sends shivers down my spine. There is no greater love than a mother; she is fierce and loyal, as seen in the goddess Kali Ma, often depicted demonic in the western world in her destroyer aspect. Yet, she is also loving and kind and the giver of life. She was the first to give us birth-death-resurrection, reminding us of our immortality and the ultimate reality that we are

---

[84] Meyer, M. W., Pagels, E. H., Robinson, J. M., Funk, W., & Poirier, P. (2009). *The Nag Hammadi Scriptures: The Revised and Updated Translation of Sacred Gnostic Texts Complete in One Volume* (1st ed.). HarperOne. (The Secret Book of John, Yaldaboath Defiles Eve (23,35-25,16) p. 128).

part of the cyclical nature of all things and not separate. Mother–God, Spirit, is a force to be reckoned with when her deep love for us helps us to break down the illusions of the ego and recognize the truth of ourselves. I have often heard, "Be careful what you ask for," because Kali Ma will come into your life and destroy everything that is not of your Divine nature to remind her children of their glory and bring them home.

Circumstances in our life may appear to be ripping us apart, but in kairos, divine timing, Mother embraces us, puts her arms out to us when we awaken to our truth and follow our soul. We did not come here to please others or do what they asked us. We came here as lightworkers to evolve humanity and raise consciousness, and we do this by following the path laid out by enlightened masters. Kali's consort is Shiva, and together they are a reminder for us to honour both the feminine and masculine aspects of ourselves. Yeshua and Miryam were a modern-day example for us of the power we all have when we harness all elements of our nature.

In this paragraph, Miryam hears the voice of Yeshua speaking to her as if from a far distance; this indicates to me that this is teaching in real-time. Not a vision of the physical Yeshua, but a deep soul connection they have, where she can perceive him with her inner eye. Yeshua is with Miryam in her heart as he guides her through her ascension, just as she was with him, through his crucifixion (detoxification), resurrection (purification) and finally his ascension, with her anointing oils. Again, as in the first chapters, he is reaffirming her as his equal, the one who knows all. Yeshua also states that he named her the Migdalah, the tower or keeper of the flocks, an authority on the teachings, capable of being a teacher and master guide. He informs us how essential her role in the ministry was and the importance of her discipleship. "I heard the voice of my master tell me, 'Miryam, whom I have called the Migdalah, now you have seen all, and have known the truth of yourself, the truth that is I AM.'"[85] Miryam has realized her I AM and has met her mirror self in the Divine. If we follow in the words of the Gospels of Thomas, she has become Yeshua's twin, and once the student has learned the truth,

---

[85] Quillan, D. J. (2010). *The Gospel of the Beloved Companion: The Complete Gospel of Mary Magdalene*. CreateSpace Independent Publishing Platform. 42:13 (page 119)

they become the teacher. This paragraph is so profound, and it shows us that Yeshua intended that Miryam would be a leader and teacher in the ministry as a completion to completions. She had reached the level of an enlightened master who would teach the inner teachings to future disciples, the way to see with our inner vision, to connect with Ascended Masters for help and support. Considering that many of the disciples of the core group (the 12 men that we know of in the canonical gospels) had not reached this level of enlightenment, it is obvious why they would fear this illuminated, empowered woman and would lay the path to eliminate her from history or silence her to the best of their ability. The teachings did not conform to their limited minds and the environment of society at the time. The women in the core group were far advanced in learning the Way that they were either silenced or presented as meek, humble, subservient witnesses to the life of Jesus, as in his mother, Mary Anna. Alternatively, they were forced to the background as silent witnesses, as in Mary Salome and Mary Clopeus.

My Soul Speaks

For this Soul speaks, I am drawn to the Secret Book of John from the Nag Hammadi Scriptures page 109, The One (2, 25-41, 19)

"The One is the immeasurable light, pure, holy, immaculate. Not that it is just perfection, or blessedness, or divinity, it is much greater.

His thought became a reality, and she who appeared in his presence in shining light came forth.

She is the first thought, the image of Spirit. She became the universal womb, for she precedes everything."[86]

We are called to live in the light of our mother within our hearts. Hear her call, release the darkness of fear, judgment, anger, hatred, and other lower-dense emotions and live in unconditional love for all of creation. It is time to bring Mother home so we may all be reunited in the holy trinity of Mother/Father/Child.

Affirmation

I intend to observe my thoughts each moment, and when I feel any dark thoughts about myself or my brothers and sisters, I will realign with my heart and recognize my error. I am not separate from the Divine love of Source or any of the world's creations.

Exercise

Mantras and visualization are powerful tools when raising our vibrational frequency. The universe consists of energy vibrations, repeating mantras identified as positive energy, opening you up to a higher dimension.

"Sadhguru is a yogi, contemporary mystic and spiritual guide. Sitting on a rock, high in the Himalayas

---

[86] Meyer, M. W., Pagels, E. H., Robinson, J. M., Funk, W., & Poirier, P. (2009). *The Nag Hammadi Scriptures: The Revised and Updated Translation of Sacred Gnostic Texts Complete in One Volume* (1st ed.). HarperOne. (The Secret Book of John, Yaldaboath Defiles Eve p. 109, The One (2, 25-41, 19)

mountains, in a place called Kantisarovar, this song was born within him.

Nada Brahma Vishwaswaroopa
Nada Hi Sakala Jeevaroopa
Nada Hi Karma Nada Hi Dharma
Nada Hi Bandhana Nada Hi Mukti
Nada Hi Shankara Nada Hi Shakti
Nadam Nadam Sarvam Nadam
Nadam Nadam Nadam Nadam

Translation: Sound is Brahman, the manifestation of the universe, sound manifests itself in the form of all life, sound is bondage, sound is the means for liberation, sound is that which binds, sound is that which liberates, sound is the bestower of all, sound is the power behind everything, sound is everything."[87] Realm of the Mystic – Sadhguru

The mantra for this meditation is Om Mani Padme Hum. This mantra invokes the unconditional love of compassion. I am particularly drawn to it because of my connection with Kuan (Guan) Yin, the Goddess of compassion. Om helps us to dissolve the ego and is the universal first sound in creation. Mani releases our attachments to physical desires and the feelings of jealousy and separation. Padme translates to lotus or wisdom and helps us cultivate connection, leaving judgements and possessive qualities. Hum releases all hatred and connects us with our innate, divine I AM presence, which cannot be disturbed by anything.

Begin in a seated position, with your hands gently in your lap. Close your eyes, set your intention, (Example: I wish to connect with the universal cosmic heart to

---

[87] Realm of the Mystic – Sadhguru

have compassion for the world's suffering, I ask for guidance in how I may be of service.)

Breathe deeply through the nose and out through the mouth, relaxing with every out-breath for around a minute or until you feel relaxed.

Begin chanting quietly, Om Mani Padme Hum; if your mind wanders, gently return to focussing on the mantra. Try this for at least 10 minutes a day. When you are ready, release the mantra and gently open your eyes.

CHAPTER 16

SILENCE SPEAKS

"Then Andrew began to speak, and said to his brothers: "Tell me, what do you think of these things she has been telling us? As for me, I do not believe that the Teacher would speak like this. These ideas are too different from those we have known." And Peter added: "How is it possible that the Teacher talked in this manner, with a woman, about secrets of which we ourselves are ignorant? Must we change our customs, and listen to this woman? Did he really choose her, and prefer her to us?"[88] (Mary 17:9-20)

A S WE DRAW TO THE FINAL VERSES OF THE VISION, WE HAVE witnessed Miryam as a woman of integrity who has taken an oath to serve humanity at the highest level of good throughout the various Nag Hammadi gospels. She is a healer and works only from the heart. She has journeyed through the darkness of her character, embraced and loved these parts of herself, and has become an enlightened being, connected with her Divine I AM presence, revealing the truth of her connection with the Divine Spirit. As she reveals to the other disciples these teachings, we cannot imagine that she would even have to say that she is telling the truth. A lie or fabrication would never be uttered from this divine-human woman in understanding her character.

---

[88] Leloup, J., Rowe, J., & Needleman, J. (2002). *The Gospel of Mary Magdalene* (First Paperback Edition). Inner Traditions. (Mary 17:9:20, page 157)

Nevertheless, Andreas (Andrew) and Shimon Kefa (Peter) accuse her of lying.

Firstly, it is not their New Testament names used in this text, which indicates it was written earlier than the canonical gospels we have today, which later translated their Hebrew names to the Greek Peter and Andrew. Second, they are challenging Miryam's integrity even though Peter previously recognized her as a favoured disciple of Yeshua and a woman who knew all whom he called sister. Attacking Miryam indicates where their state of consciousness is, not nearly as advanced as Miryam's. They missed the mark (sin) and had not fully integrated the message of unconditional love. These teachings were far too different, which confirms for us that Yeshua did not feel they were ready for the more profound, inner teachings; they had not reached the level of awareness required to move to the next level lessons.

Lastly, both of these disciples are recorded as the first disciples in the canonical gospels, yet even after years with Yeshua and his ministry of equality, they are still attached to their patriarchal Judaic past and unable to see and understand the teachings, especially from a mere woman. So here we see the first accurate picture we receive as to the split in Christianity and the formation of an all-male Church that denigrates the female race and silences her.

The gospels speak of Miryam becoming silent after disclosing this teaching to the disciples, as this is where Yeshua spoke with her. It is in the silence of dropping into our hearts, clearing the chatter from our minds, where we can encounter divine guidance. As we recall, when she had fully ascended, the physical world became silent; she could no longer hear the incessant chatter and callings of the ego/false self. The Church teaches rehearsed and memorized prayer, Yeshua taught silence, go within and be pure of heart, Divine Mother/Father knows our hearts and hears our prayers through the silence. The eye of the heart, encountering visions of the Divine from within, is the true meaning of those with the eyes to see and the ears to hear – the inner voice of our true selves will remember the truth. We know that Yeshua spoke in parables; he knew each disciple could understand different levels depending on their state of consciousness. The disciples who would understand the parables would become teachers to future followers of the outer way; they would be able to speak at the level of the masses. A disciple of Miryam's enlightenment would turn many people away from the movement; they would not understand the level of awareness she was speaking. Miryam was a teacher of the further developed disciples, the ones who were ready to perceive with their inner eye of the heart. The disciples who were not at the same capacity of peace, unable to connect with their inner vision, would think this is all in her imagination. Yeshua would have guided each of them according to their degree of understanding. Some disciples would be acquainted with parables, the most basic foundational teachings, while more advanced disciples would have achieved a greater understanding of the more profound inner work. As previously discussed, Miryam, Thomas and Phillip appear to have reached Yeshua's unity consciousness. The more evolved students would be open to spiritual vision; Miryam was one of the refined students. Yeshua continually praises her for being diligent in her studies and spiritual practices. As we saw earlier, this praise caused much friction among the other male disciples, most notably Peter. Peter could not change his customs from his Judaic patriarchal upbringing to accept that a mere woman had access to their teacher's more profound spiritual teachings. The societal norms of women being a lesser species were also ingrained in the Jewish religion; women were to be subservient to men. She was created after Adam to satisfy all his needs while he led the world; many of the male disciples, no matter how much they learned from Yeshua, could not release these prejudices.

The Western churches of the day were all pomp and showmanship, males strutting about acting as the authority of their all-male God. Miryam knew it was in the silence where the good found her, and she discovered her divine self. Yeshua empowered the women followers, and this made many of the male disciples uncomfortable. Yeshua's ministry was one of equality, and the women were prominent ministers when the teachings were held in private homes. Female leaders flourished in the early church up until the fourth century; we see this in the letters of Paul, as well as many gnostic texts. Pauls's letter to Timothy is a statement that has been debated upon for centuries, "A woman should learn in quietness and full submission. I do not permit a woman to teach or to assume authority over a man; she must be quiet."[89] (1 Tim 2:11-12). Paul wrote a personal letter to his friend Timothy concerning a specific issue he was dealing with at his church in Ephesus of false teachings, not to the Universal Church. When writing his letter, the worship of the goddess Cybele (Artemis by the Greeks) was practiced in violent rituals against men symbolizing the murder of the false god Attis. Male priests were being castrated, renouncing sex in honour of Cybele and Attis during these demonic rituals. In the fourth century, when St. Jerome worked on translating the bible to Latin, gender bias translations were introduced, words and complete passages were changed to reduce the influence of females in the church. Jerome was a strict patriarchal Roman who often spoke of women as being evil. Throughout the book of Acts and his letters, Paul says highly of the female ministers; it is unlikely he would write to Timothy that females should not teach. It is more likely; his letter indicated that women should not have domination over men but should learn the truth and teach only Yeshua's message. St. Jerome most likely altered this passage in his Latin translation.

When Constantine adopted Christianity as the new Roman universal religion in the fourth century, the empire had always functioned as an honour-shame culture; the Romans conquered and dominated to maintain power and control. The majority of people were merely trying to survive; after paying their taxes to support the richness of the Roman empire, there was very little left for food or housing. We have already discussed the role of women in the Roman hierarchy, way down at the bottom with the slaves. Anyone who threatened this hierarchy was persecuted, tried and crucified. By the time Constantine became Emperor, the Roman empire was crumbling, he was desperate to maintain control, and the only way the Romans knew was through fear and domination. Constantine signed a proclamation that prohibited the persecution of Christians and institutionalized the church. When this happened, male government officials were made bishops, and the church became a mirror of the same hierarchy witnessed in Roman society. A structure of authority was implemented, women were silenced.

---

[89] Haynes, C. L., Jr, Haynes, C. L., Jr, Baker, L. L., & Danzey, E. (n.d.). *The Bible - Read and Study Free Online*. Bible Study Tools. Retrieved January 5, 2021, from https://www.biblestudytools.com/1 Tim 2:11-12

Unfortunately, from the second century onwards, so many inspiring books were condemned as heretical, either destroyed by fire or, as we are recently discovering, buried deep in the desert. The Acts of Paul and Thecla are inspiring and empowering for all women. Thecla, an independent, outspoken young woman who travelled dressed as a man and preached the good news, was a role model for many women in early Christianity. The Dialogue of the Saviour, Sophia of Jesus Christ, The Pistis Sophia and The Gospel of Phillip are all apocryphal works that give us a clearer picture of Miryam's prominence in the early Christian movement. Her spiritual perfection is captured in each of these testaments. Miryam was a prophetic visionary and elevated leader among the disciples. She is now speaking louder than any other disciple from her silence, and it is time we all listen.

My Soul Speaks

It is all a story; it is not who we are. I am pure love, on a journey to awaken to what that love is. Every person you encounter is a teacher, and every experience is teaching; there are angels and ascended masters always guiding us to return home to the silence and listen to the soft whispers. Miryam is calling for you to awaken fully to your divine self.

Affirmation

I am one with the infinite joy, peace and abundance of the Universe. Therefore, in silence and contemplation, I move forward wholly in the present moment and know that the Divine guides every step.

Exercise

If possible, step outside and look around at your surroundings – see the abundance of the Universe. List at least five things you see that proclaim the abundant nature of Infinite Love – the trees, the leaves on the trees, chirping birds.

Sit on the grass and feel Mother Earth beneath you, breathe in deeply, with trust and faith that She is holding you, you are safe and secure. Then, either with your eyes open or closed, continue to breathe in complete silence. If words or thoughts cross your mind, smile, thank them and let them go. Do not judge them or become frustrated; just let go. The more you practice the silence, the easier it will become, and the less your mind will distract you. If you have a specific prayer for guidance, you can ask for direction and then listen in the silence for the answer. It may not come to you immediately but be on the lookout for signs throughout the day; prayers are always answered. The Divine answers in some of the most peculiar yet spectacular ways have no expectations or specific outcomes.

CHAPTER 17

THE GREAT DIVIDE

I N THE FOLLOWING VERSES, WE SEE THE HURT MIRYAM FEELS FROM the male disciples believing that she could lie to them about Yeshua, her beloved Rabbi and companion, and again insists that she speaks only the truth.

"Then Mary wept and answered him: "My brother Peter, what can you be thinking? Do you believe that this is just my own imagination, that I invented this vision? Or do you believe that I would lie about our Teacher?"[90] (Mary 18:1-6)

Miryam has been a beloved disciple from the beginning with Shimon Kefa; they have walked alongside one another, and Yeshua listening to his words, absorbing his teachings. One thing that is very transparent here is that Yeshua only shared these teachings with Miryam as he knew the purity of her heart and her readiness for her ascension. This most profound teaching was not one to be taken lightly, for anyone who was not yet ready would be unequipped for the bright light of their divine selves. Gnosis (inner knowledge) is only revealed when we are prepared to receive it, through a pure heart, and only by Divine grace. This teaching was reserved for the very advanced disciple whom Yeshua believed was ready to become his equal, who had integrated the way within their hearts, lived-in authenticity and truth, and were prepared to teach it to other advanced students. From this, we can see that many of the male disciples had not achieved the level of mastery required and

---

[90] Leloup, J., Rowe, J., & Needleman, J. (2002). *The Gospel of Mary Magdalene* (First Paperback Edition). Inner Traditions. (Mary 18:1-6 page 165)

were therefore not taught these secret inner teachings. We can also see that Andreas and Shimon Kefa still held jealousy, envy and hatred in their hearts; they had not even achieved the root of the teaching, release all judgement and wrath and live with love and compassion. Peter, the disciple, is the one who is honoured with the title of the founder of Christianity as we know it today, the rock upon which the church was built. He was a disciple who was not a master of the actual teachings of Yeshua and certainly did not understand the depths of the message of what Yeshua taught. This hatred and anger were infused into the Church and has created great suffering for humanity.

Next, we see that Levi defends Miryam and indicates her importance amongst the disciples and to Yeshua. Finally, Levi reprimands the others and reminds them of her achievement of completion as a fully realized human.

Levi said to Peter, "Peter, you are always ready to give way to your perpetual inclination to anger. And even now, you are doing exactly that by questioning the woman as though you're her adversary."[91] (Mary 10:7-8) and "If the Savior considered her to be worthy, who are you to disregard her? For he knew her completely and loved her steadfastly."[92] (Mary 10:9-10)

In Levi's defence of Miryam, we catch a glimpse into the nature of Shimon Kefa as a "Hot-tempered" man. This is not a peaceful disciple capable of teaching the world about love and compassion. We also receive another testament about how Yeshua felt about Miryam, worthy of being a leader and his companion whom he knew better than any other and loved most of all. This is again a testament to his humanity; he could love all creation but had a human tendency to have a deeper, more profound, intimate love for one woman, Miryam. We have discussed the probability of a marriage between Yeshua and Miryam, and this paragraph confirms their deep connection at both a physical and profoundly spiritual level. It is explainable by the Church that Yeshua could have been celibate as a man, but it would have been unacceptable for women to travel amongst men who were not related

---

[91] Watterson, M. (2021). *Mary Magdalene Revealed: The First Apostle, Her Feminist Gospel & the Christianity We Haven't Tried Yet* (2nd ed.). Hay House Inc.(page 191)
[92] Ibid 91. (Page 203)

to them. We already know the other Mary's mentioned in the canonical gospels were all related to Yeshua (his mother, aunt and cousin), except Mary Magdalene; sometimes the unspoken words are more meaningful than the spoken ones. Miryam would have faced death by stoning, a single woman amongst strange men travelling the hostile roads of Israel. This depiction alone would have condemned her, especially the Rabbi, who knew her better than all other women. He loved her more than the other disciples because she was a master who achieved enlightenment and because she was his Spiritual partner, his companion, his wife.

Now we see Levi telling the followers precisely what this woman has achieved and that they must do as their Rabbi said and go out and spread the good news exactly as it was taught to them.

"We should clothe ourselves with the perfect Human, acquire it for ourselves as he commanded us, and announce the Good news."[93] (Mary 10:11-13)

Miryam is a fully enlightened master who has achieved perfect humanity. Levi tells them they would be wise to acquire the same level of humanity that she has already obtained and look to her as an example. The Disciples are reminded that he instructed them not to create any new rules or laws other than those he taught. We know from the New Testament that the Church fathers made several new rules and laws; approximately 1,050 commands are written in the New Testament for Christians to obey. From the Christian assemblies of Australia, a document listing the orders and, due to repetition, they have classified them under 800 headings. See abc.net.au for a complete list of the paper. They state that "They cover every phase of man's life in his relationship to God, and his fellowmen, now and hereafter. If obeyed, they will bring rich rewards here and forever; if disobeyed, they will bring condemnation and eternal punishment."[94] The document is broken down by what to abstain, avoid, ask, be, be not's, be wares, consider whom to honour, and on for twelve pages. With this overwhelming list of commands, it is no surprise that the people felt and still do to

---

[93] Ibid:91. (Page 213)

[94] Christian Assemblies International. (2011, April). *ABC (Australian Broadcasting Corporation)*. Https://Www.Abc.Net.Au/Reslib/201407/R1308729_17984331. Pdf. https://www.abc.net.au/reslib/201407/r1308729_17984331.pdf

this day, that they had to attend confession; it would be impossible to achieve perfect humanity under these unachievable demands; humanity has been perpetually living with guilt and shame, stifling our evolution. Thousands of years of oppression convinced us we are all condemned to eternal punishment! At each of the boughs of the tree described in the Gospel of the Beloved Companion and The Gospel of Mary Magdalene, we get clear and concise practices, straightforward ways of living. As we begin to be aware of our thoughts and actions, regularly and relentlessly observe each time we digress into lower ego desires, the reward is power and healing for ourselves, our families and all creation. The Divine graces us with light, goodness and beauty in our hearts. Yeshua and Miryam's simple way of living, the way of the heart, became convoluted and rigid, filled with rules and commands, a select group of pious priests and clergy demanded of their congregations. These unattainable commands have led to civilization's digression, a global pandemic of living only for ourselves, inflating our egos and forgetting our true humanity as both a physical body and a soul. The Good news the disciples were commanded to spread was that the kingdom's treasure was within us all along.

The great divide in Christianity began as soon as Yeshua departed from them. As the disciples parted ways to go and teach the gospel, each took a different level of knowledge, ranging from the essential "act as Yeshua acted" to the more profound inner teachings of vision. The Christianity of the East significantly differs from one of the Western worlds; this was entirely dependent on which disciple went where with their either limited or extensive gnosis. Today, we have over 45,000 denominations of Christianity globally. Initially, the split was believed to be based on opposing views of whether Jesus was "begotten" by God, or God incarnate, debated in the fourth century. Still, the recent discoveries of lost texts suggest this split happened from the very beginning. According to Mary's gospel, this split occurred when many male disciples discredited her revelation of a vision from within. Interestingly, often when I would share a message I received from a loved one who crossed over, I was also met with doubt, "Why would he/she come to you and not me/us?" This is ego speaking, and the vision comes to those who are open to receive.

CHAPTER 18

THE ESSENE TEACHINGS

I N 1928 EDMOND BORDEAUX SZEKELY PUBLISHED THE FIRST VOLUME of the *Essene Gospel of Peace*. The English version was published in 1937. He had found this ancient manuscript, written in Aramaic in the Secret Archives of the Vatican. Another copy exists in Old Slavonic in the Royal Library of the Hapsburgs in Vienna (now the property of the Austrian government). Books Two and Three, *The Unknown Books of the Essenes* and *Lost Scrolls of The Essene Brotherhood* were published fifty years after the first French translation of 1928. In 1981 Book Four, *The Teachings of the Elect* was published at his request two years after his death.[95] www.essene.com

The Essenes existed before Yeshua arrived in the body on Earth, and I believe he was a Son of Light. They thrived from around the second century BCE to the first century CE, when the Romans destroyed them in 68 CE. Many scholars believe these translations by Edmond are a forgery. However, we have seen many non-Christian leaders had the wherewithal to hide their writings in jars and bury them deep in the Earth in caves. I include the following texts from the Essene Gospel of Peace because it is genuinely relevant to the world today. The Elders warn that the Son of Man will betray his mother, and the world will be thrown into darkness; our hunger and greed will destroy the Earth. This Gospel also informs us of the laws of the Universe; it is our responsibility

---

[95] Christ, J., & Szekely, E. B. (2016). *The Essene Gospel of Peace - Book Four: The Teachings of the Elect.* ⌐International Biogenic Society; Not Indicated edition (January 1, 1981).

to learn and care for our Earthly Mother and see her beauty and grace even in the 'smallest drop of dew,' appreciate and have gratitude for every living thing. Lastly, it also reminds us of who we are; we are light, life and sound. When we die, our bodies will return to the Earth, but our essence will return to our Heavenly Father. When we consider that this book was written around the same time as Yeshua lived and taught, it is much older than the New Testament writings. This is a testament to what we have witnessed in our world for the past few thousand years.

Book Four: The Teachings of the Elect

> An Elder speaking to the assembled Brothers who have been through a seven-year preparation.
>
> "But there will come a day when the Son of Man will turn his face from his Earthly Mother and betray her, even denying his Mother and his birthright. Then shall he sell her into slavery, and her flesh shall be ravaged, her blood polluted, and her breath smothered; he will bring the fire of death into all the parts of her kingdom, and his hunger will devour all her gifts and leave in their place only a desert.
>
> "All these things he will do out of ignorance of the Law, and as a man dying slowly cannot smell his own stench, so will the Son of Man be blind to the truth: that as he plunders and ravages and destroys his Earthly Mother, so does he plunder and ravage and destroy himself. For he was born of his Earthly Mother, and he is one with her, and all that he does to his Mother even so does he do to himself." (362)
>
> "Only when he returns to the bosom of his Earthly Mother will he find everlasting life and the Stream of Life which leads to his Heavenly Father; only then may the dark vision of the future come not to pass."[96] (372)

---

[96] Ibid:95.

We recall that Malachi quoted in his book St. Mary Magdalene, from the Gospel of the Sophia Ain Sof, that it is only through receiving the Mother Spirit back into our hearts that we will heal. The Essene

Gospel of Peace predictions written 2,000 years ago is precisely what we are witnessing on our planet right now. We are destroying Mother Earth, and as we do so, we are also leading ourselves farther away from the paradise promised us by our Heavenly Father. In uniting our creators' masculine and feminine aspects within our hearts, we will conquer the dense darkness and live our full humanity as children of divine light.

CONCLUSION

MY HOPE IN WRITING THIS IS A DEEP LONGING FOR A MORE loving, compassionate and gentler world where all creation will once again live in harmony and peace, where the highest good for all is always our primary focus. I believe deep in my bones that I am called to awaken my priestess's ancestral codes and be empowered now to exercise my gifts of healing to the world. My soul desire, the reason for being embodied as a female at this time, I believe, is to share the story of female oppression, both in my personal life, the lives of women I have known in this incarnation, and our ancestors. I am informed about healing these wounds in my own heart and those around me to help birth the new Earth. As the human race, the grandest of Infinite Source creations, we require a complete spiritual overhaul. The Gospel of the Beloved Companion, the complete Gospels of Mary Magdalene, and the Gospel of Mary Magdalene is a blueprint for this change, left for us over 2,000 years ago by the great Ascended Masters Jesus and Mary, the humans Yeshua and Miryam, who lived virtuous lives, achieved enlightenment and ascended into their full humanity and divinity while incarnated on the Earth realm. Yeshua was adamant in all of the gospels, canonical and apocryphal, that he did not want worship; only one born not of a woman, the Creator of all, deserves our reverence. These teachings call for humanity to let go of everything we have been taught thus far, be open-minded, and embrace the mystery. Western society is caught up in the patriarchal, chronological, rational mind (the head-brain). Miryam's secret teaching asks us to release these limiting beliefs, open ourselves up to the unknown, the realm of inner vision and trust our intuition, where miracles are to be found. Are some of these teachings woo-woo, as my Christian friends called them? This depends entirely on our perception, and inner vision is not open for debate, defence or discussion; it is unique and individual, just as every one of us is. The whole point is not to follow the status quo but to be as outrageously distinct and eccentric as possible and contribute to everything in our own way. Here we live the whole life imaginable, as our authentic, beautiful selves.

The Church has focused so much attention on Jesus' death, Christians wear the cross as a badge of honour to declare their faith, but it was the example of how to live that was the most critical part of Yeshua and Miryam's mission. Living for Spirit, the Good is our true salvation. If we live only to fulfill Divine Will, we honour our Earthly Mother and our Heavenly Father, and we walk the path of love. Yeshua and Miryam walked the way of the heart in every act in their life to show all of us how to attain Christ's consciousness. Humanity faces a precipice; we can begin to raise awareness and consciousness or end our reign here on this earth and take everything down with us. It is time for a new earth, and we must now recognize that we are children of the light and goodness and create harmony and peace in our world. To achieve this, we must create a new Christian story that includes both the feminine and masculine aspects. We must put the same amount of emphasis on the order of the Marys', the order of the blue rose, and their significant contribution to the ministry as we have the male disciples. Miryam is one of the only disciples identified in any of the writings we currently have that has embraced and completed the teachings of both the inner and outer traditions, the purification of her soul as a completion to completions. She achieved Divine union and was a powerful healer and, more, a manifest vessel of divine love in the same realization as Yeshua. The Church teaches of the second coming of Christ. I do not believe that this second coming is a person, it will be when enough of the world's population awakens into Christ's consciousness, and we can move from this three-dimensional, dense existence into a higher dimension of living from our light bodies. Emanating only light and goodness and recognizing this light in all of creation. The truth of Oneness is rooted in love and union, union within us, our fellow beings, creation and cooperation with the Divine. Living from the heart in complete surrender to guidance from our higher selves, releasing all fear, doubt, hatred and anger, replacing these emotions with love and compassion for all of creation is the path to becoming a living light. These teachings are a radical change from the outer God–hero to the inner divine in the heart of each of us.

Once we have descended to the depths of our shadows, felt our humanity fully and transformed our darkness with love, we can then release our attachments to the ego and not be enslaved by their powers. Forgiveness is one of the most critical messages, my journey into my heart had to begin with forgiving myself. I had to release an ancient belief system ingrained in my subconscious that I was flawed, unworthy, born of original sin, and continually remind myself I am pure of heart. I also had to forgive the thousands of years of oppression of the feminine, which led to the denigration of living females. So, if there is anything you take from these writings, start with forgiveness and a pure heart.

As we realize our humanity is an opportunity for us to express divine love in this dense atmosphere of the physical world, start to hear with our inner ears, and see our inner sight, life will begin to flow through us. Once we awaken to more than the reality of our five sensory perceptions, we can "hear" and "see" divine guidance through grace. No longer limited to this three-dimensional reality, we can discover the "many mansions" Yeshua spoke of in his "Fathers" house. We belong to a vast, multidimensional universe, where time and space are constructs of this egoic reality. The flesh is a temporary vessel that allows us to carry out our souls' purpose on the earth realm; the realization of our interconnectedness with all creation, our divinity is the whole point of being human. Our souls can choose to remain free of the body in blissful limitlessness, but we will not evolve; our purpose is to have this experience and share everything we learn. A human experience allows us to choose divine love no matter what. We will all have moments of despair, hurt, betrayal, loss of loved ones; each moment is another chance to encounter the grace of Infinite Love, to choose love over bitterness, joy over anger or sadness. The heart is a path to cultivate inner strength, embrace our humanity, and remember we are also a soul, so in the middle of the pain and darkness, love remains in our hearts when even the unimaginable can happen.

My kids were telling me about a Twitter survey that asked women what they would do if all men were removed from the Earth for 24 hours. The answers were universal; most said they would go for walks at 3 am, go to clubs until the wee hours of the morning, wear revealing clothing without fear or shame, not lock their doors. This indicates where humanity is currently residing in a dark and dense world. The fact that young women have so much fear of their brothers is disconcerting. Young women fear because the Church and society have taught for thousands of years that females are a lesser species who must be subservient to the males, whether that was her father, brother or husband. Yeshua and Miryam showed us a profoundly loving, equal partnership of males and females, as well as the importance of uniting the masculine and feminine natures within our hearts.

Once our Holy Mother is honoured and revered in the same fashion as our Divine Father has been over the centuries, when reunited in the hearts of humanity, a world of love and light will emerge. However, until there is balance within each of us of both our masculine and feminine natures, we will continue on this dark path to extinction. Therefore, the balance is of paramount importance now!

Yeshua and Miryam were here to heal the world, free us from our attachment to the ego and demonstrated through action how we could achieve peace in this lifetime, regardless of what is happening in the outside world, by immersing ourselves on the path inward. They taught, our colour, race, the unique physical qualities each of us possess is a testament to the creativity of our Divine Mother/Father. We owe it to them to share our creativity freely with all humanity equally. Life would be boring if we only had one bird species, reptile, flower. We glory at the colours in nature; we should also revere the colours and uniqueness of every human.

Some of my testimonies may seem heartbreaking to a few, while others may feel they have been dealt a more tragic hand in this lifetime. Wherever you are on your journey of discovery is exactly where you are meant to be. No one is better than the other; we are all teachers and students at all times. Listen, learn and grow from everyone you encounter; the Universe is always speaking to us. I share my stories as a reminder, no matter what we have been through or are going through, we always have a choice (free will) to return to love over fear, the love that transcends death. The visions I have experienced in this embodiment may be interpreted as grandiose to some readers, arrogant even. However, the various translations of Mary's Gospels remind us that this is our natural state and the only way for humanity to grow into our highest potential. When we purify our heart, connect with our higher selves, limitless, eternal soul or the nous, the bridge that marries us to Spirit, we are graced with visions and messages that will guide us in evolving our planet. The beliefs of the past twenty centuries are crumbling; the linear, rational, thinking, intensely masculine mind is ready to marry the kind, compassionate, allowing, feminine heart. Be open and gentle; the bride is returning and reuniting with her beloved, which is the path home to ourselves.

All my love, always.

ACKNOWLEDGMENTS

I HAVE HAD MANY DIFFICULT MOMENTS IN THIS INCARNATION, BUT I have had many more joyous and beautiful times. I want to thank our Holy Mother and Divine Father for their infinite love and gift of life. I thank them for the lessons to nudge my spiritual evolution and, in deep reverence, honour the life I am living. I am humbled in their presence; it is only them I hope I have pleased in writing this; only their authority matters. Deeply grateful to the humans, Yeshua and Miryam, the ascended masters, Jesus and Mary Magdalene, who showed us a better way to be human. Thank you for sharing the potential within each of us to do better and for the example of a divinely guided relationship with ourselves and our fellow creatures. Thank you.

I would also like to thank the many authors, scholars, theologians who have inspired me to search for deeper meaning and truth. Jehanne De Quillan, for translating and sharing the beautiful gospel, The Gospel of the Beloved Companion, The Complete Gospels of Mary Magdalene, when humanity was in desperate need of it. Meggan Watterson was the first to wake me out of my slumber with her book Revealed, The Gospel of Mary. I recall crying and fist-pumping a resounding Yes! Yes! Yes! I am forever in your debt for validating my place in the world as a woman. Cynthia Bourgeault, Jean Yves-Leloupe, Margaret Starbird, Carolynn Myss are many of the authors who contributed to my thirst for more answers to know the real Yeshua and Miryam. Thank you.

Deep gratitude to my brother Reverend Danny for our weekly spiritual discussions; you were my first friend and continue to be a pillar of faith for your entire family and community. Also, my heart circle, who raise my vibration every Thursday morning, with their insights, suggestions and highly qualified information, from social media, marketing, NFTs and of course, spiritual development. From this group, I would especially like to thank my dear friend of twenty-eight years, Bill Wilson, for his mentorship and the occasional kick in the ass when I procrastinated. Also, Dave Rogers, who is new to my life but has had an incredible impact in a few short months, I am learning to speak my truth with his way of making me get uncomfortable. He also read one of the final drafts and offered his input; I appreciate you.

Rising Angels, a local not-for-profit organization that educates and advocates for the victims of human trafficking in Canada. Katarina Macleod, the Executive Director, has become a dear friend to me and a second Mama to our daughter. She is an incredible woman who gives selflessly, helping victims to learn how to value themselves, shows them their worthiness and is a constant reminder of the divine feminine in action. You are my hero Kat.

Last but not least, my family, my husband Don and my children, Christopher, Jonathan and Alexis, your patience while I was writing and listening to my paragraphs over and over were crucial in the development of this book. I often joked that it would amaze people to know I wrote at the kitchen table. At the same time, simultaneously, four other adults played their music from different rooms, the television was on, and my boys were yelling at a Liverpool game. I learned from a young age to tune out everything around me and go into silence. So, thank you for pressing pause and sharing in my excitement.

BIBLIOGRAPHY

Bourgeault, C. (2017, April 20). *Be Whole Hearted*. Cac.Org. https://cac. org/be-whole-hearted-2017-04-20/

Christ, J., & Szekely, E. B. (2016). *The Essene Gospel of Peace - Book Four: The Teachings of the Elect*. International Biogenic Society; Not Indicated edition (January 1, 1981).

Christian Assemblies International. (2011, April). *ABC (Australian Broadcasting Corporation)*. Https://Www.Abc.Net.Au/Reslib/201407/ R1308729_17984331.Pdf. https://www.abc.net.au/reslib/201407/ r1308729_17984331.pdf

Contributors to Wikimedia projects. (2020, December 28). *Anthropos*. Wikipedia. https://en.wikipedia.org/wiki/Anthropos

Foundation For Inner Peace. (1992). *A Course in Miracles, Combined Volume: Text, Workbook for Students, Manual for Teachers, 2nd Edition* (2nd ed.). Foundation for Inner Peace.

Haynes, C. L., Jr, Haynes, C. L., Jr, Baker, L. L., & Danzey, E. (n.d.). *The Bible - Read and Study Free Online*. Bible Study Tools. Retrieved January 5, 2021, from https://www.biblestudytools.com/

HeartMath Institute. (2020, December 20). *Science of the Heart*. https:// www.heartmath.org/research/science-of-the-heart/

Klingler, S. A., & Taylor, S. A. (2017). *The Akashic Tarot: A 62-card Deck and Guidebook* (Tcr Crds/P ed.). Hay House Inc.

Leloup, J. (2006). *The Sacred Embrace of Jesus and Mary: The Sexual Mystery at the Heart of the Christian Tradition* (Translation ed.). Inner Traditions.

Leloup, J., Rowe, J., & Needleman, J. (2002). *The Gospel of Mary Magdalene* (First Paperback Edition). Inner Traditions.

Leloup, J., Rowe, J., & Needleman, J. (2004). *The Gospel of Philip: Jesus, Mary Magdalene, and the Gnosis of Sacred Union* (Illustrated ed.). Inner Traditions.

Malachi, T. (2006). *St. Mary Magdalene: The Gnostic Tradition of the Holy Bride (Gnostic (4))* (First Edition). Llewellyn Publications.

Meyer, M. W., & Boer, E. D. A. (2006). *The Gospels of Mary: The Secret Tradition of Mary Magdalene, the Companion of Jesus*. HarperOne.

Meyer, M. W., Pagels, E. H., Robinson, J. M., Funk, W., & Poirier, P. (2009). *The Nag Hammadi Scriptures: The Revised and Updated Translation of Sacred Gnostic Texts Complete in One Volume* (1st ed.). HarperOne.

Myss, C. (1996). *Anatomy of the Spirit: The Seven Stages of Power and Healing* (1st ed.). Harmony.

Norwich, J. O. (2020). *Revelations of Divine Love by Julian of Norwich*. Independently published.

Parrott, D.M., ed. *Nag Hammadi Codices III,3–4 and V,1 with Papyrus Berolinensis 8502,3 and Oxyrhynchus Papyrus 1081: Eugnostos and the Sophia of Jesus Christ*. NHS 27. Leiden/New York: Brill, 1991 100, 4

Priaulx, O., & de Beauvoir Priaulx, O. (2015). *The Indian Travels of Apollonius of Tyana*. Fb&c Limited.

Prophet, E. C. (1958). Summit Lighthouse. Https://Www.Summitlighthouse. Org. https://www.summitlighthouse.org/violet-flame/

Quillan, D. J. (2010). *The Gospel of the Beloved Companion: The Complete Gospel of Mary Magdalene*. CreateSpace Independent Publishing Platform.

Realist, V. A. P. B. T. C. (2018, April 8). *How did we get the name Jesus when the Letter "J" didn't exist in Jesus' time?* The Christian Realist. https://thechristianrealistcom.wordpress.com/2018/04/02/how-did-we-get-the-name-jesus-when-the-letter-j-didnt-exist-in-jesus-time/

Schucman, H. (2017). *COURSE IN MIRACLES: Based On The Original Handwritten Notes Of Helen Schucman--Complete & Annotated Edition*. Circle of Atonement.

Starbird, M. (2009). *Sacred Union in Christianity*. Margaretstarbird.Net. http://margaretstarbird.net

Starr, M. (2019). *Wild Mercy: Living the Fierce and Tender Wisdom of the Women Mystics*. Sounds True.

Syswerda, J. E. (2018). *Women of the Bible: 52 Bible Studies for Individuals and Groups*. HarperChristian Resources.

Thiering, B. (1992). *Jesus & the Riddle of the Dead Sea Scrolls: Unlocking the Secrets of His Life Story* (1st HarperCollins ed). HarperCollins.

Tree of Life. (n.d.). *Tree of Life - A Thorough Explanation*. Token Rock. Retrieved February 1, 2021, from https://www.tokenrock.com/explain-tree-of-life-160.html

Virtue, D. (2004). *Goddess Guidance Oracle Cards* (Box ed.). Hay House Inc.

Watterson, M. (2021). *Mary Magdalene Revealed: The First Apostle, Her Feminist Gospel & the Christianity We Haven't Tried Yet* (2nd ed.). Hay House Inc.

Watterson, M. (2018). *The Divine Feminine Oracle: A 53-Card Deck & Guidebook for Embodying Love* (Crds ed.). Hay House Inc.

Printed in the United States
by Baker & Taylor Publisher Services